Making the Most of
Your Child's Learning Style

Every Child Can Succeed

Cynthia Ulrich Tobias

PUBLISHING
Colorado Springs, Colorado

EVERY CHILD CAN SUCCEED
Copyright © 1996 by Cynthia Ulrich Tobias, M.Ed. All rights reserved. International copyright secured.

Library of Congress Cataloging-in-Publication Data
Tobias, Cynthia Ulrich, 1953–
    Every child can succeed : Making the most of your child's learning style / Cynthia Ulrich Tobias.
        p.   c.m.
    Includes bibliographical references (p.).
    ISBN 1-56179-462-7
    1. Individualized instruction.   2. Cognitive styles in children.   I. Title.
LB1031.T63   1996
371.3'94—dc20   96-10536
                                                                 CIP

Published by Focus on the Family Publishing, Colorado Springs, Colorado 80995.

Distributed in the U.S.A. and Canada by Word Books, Dallas, Texas.

The terms *Concrete Sequential, Abstract Sequential, Abstract Random,* and *Concrete Random* are used with the permission of Anthony F. Gregorc, Ph.D. Mind Styles™ is a trademark of Anthony F. Gregorc, Ph.D.

No part of this publication may be reproduced, stored in a retrieval system, or transmitted in any form or by any means—electronic, mechanical, photocopy, recording, or otherwise—without prior permission of the publisher.

Focus on the Family books are available at special quantity discounts when purchased in bulk by corporations, organizations, churches, or groups. Special imprints, messages, and excerpts can be produced to meet your needs. For more information, write: Special Sales Department, Focus on the Family Publishing, 8605 Explorer Drive, Colorado Springs, CO 80920; or call (719) 531-3400 and ask for the Special Sales Department.

Editor: Michele A. Kendall
Designer: BC Studios
Cover Design: Bradley Lind
Cover Illustrations: Ron Wheeler

Printed in the United States of America

96 97 98 99 00 01 02 03/10 9 8 7 6 5 4 3 2 1

Dedication

This book is dedicated to my parents,
Robert and Minnie Ulrich. Although they had
every reason to be frustrated with me—their headstrong,
restless, unpredictable daughter—their love, patience,
and encouragement brought out the best in me.
Their example is the best legacy
I can pass on to my own children.

Table of Contents

Preface

For every parent who has experienced frustration with his or her children, I believe this book will provide some of the best advice you'll ever get. In order to get the most out of what you're about to read, however, it's important to keep in mind the following two statements:

1. Often the characteristics and behaviors that annoy us most about our children will be the qualities that make them successful as adults. You may feel your child talks too much or moves too much or takes too many chances, and yet those are some of the traits that are consistently found in successful entrepreneurs and business leaders. Although you must maintain bottom-line accountability and discipline, remember that the children who may be most inconvenient for you now may, when they grow up, turn out to be the best thing that ever happened to this world.

2. The quality of the relationship you have with each child will determine the effectiveness of the techniques you use. If you have cultivated a loving and healthy relationship with each of your children, they will care very much about preserving it. If there is no benefit in keeping the parental relationship intact, your efforts to discipline and motivate may have little or no effect. Even the child with the strongest will responds more to love and genuine kindness than to creative or flashy methods and approaches.

Much of what you read in this book will validate what you've believed in your heart all along. I did not make up any of these concepts; they're all based on solid, empirical research. As you read these pages, you'll come to realize that both you *and* your children are unique and wonderful individuals with great strengths and promise.

Enjoy this book. It may be the best thing that has happened to your family in a long time.

Acknowledgments

I would like to gratefully acknowledge my husband, John, for his tireless support as working husband and Mr. Mom; my treasured friends and colleagues Carol Funk and Kathy Koch, for their invaluable advice and critique; my secretary and dear friend Darlene Fleutsch, for her dedication and zeal; and Gwen Ellis, my first editor, for taking my talent and inspiring me to become a writer.

Chapter One

How Can Such a Wonderful Kid Cause So Much Stress?

"Why can't you just do what you're told?"

"*Look* at me when I'm talking to you!"

"This room is a *mess!*"

"You just don't appreciate what you have."

"Kids! They think they know it all—you can't tell them *anything!*"

"You'd better watch your attitude!"

As a parent, you know that each of your children is a God-given gift with special talents and unique and wonderful characteristics. But let's face it—the same child who gives you so much joy can also be your greatest challenge. In fact, you may have noticed that every child in your family presents a *different* challenge. How can children growing up in the same home with the same parents be so diverse? Why don't your children automatically deal with the world in the same way you do? Do they *deliberately* annoy you? Are they *trying* to drive you crazy?

Over the years, researchers have discovered many of the reasons each person is unique. There are so many pieces to this puzzle that for some people, the issue has become too complex. Researchers have identified several personality types, at least four different temperaments, and many diverse management and teaching styles.

If it sounds overwhelming, it can be. But this book is here to offer you hope. Most busy parents, even when motivated, can't spare the time to delve into ponderous academic literature, only to find they'll have to dig out any practical nuggets for themselves. Ironically, many researchers of individual differences seem convinced that their model is the only one a person would need. Therefore, as you study a researcher's work and approach, you'll feel a need to "fit" yourself neatly into one of the categories. Even when the research and methods are sound, many who try to understand the theory give up in frustration when it comes to putting it into practice.

In my first book, *The Way They Learn*, I introduced five different research models in the field of learning styles—inborn strengths and characteristics possessed by every individual.[1] If personality and temperament are some of the most significant portions of each person's puzzle, then learning styles are the pieces that make up the border. (See puzzle diagram on p. 24.) Your learning style determines what makes sense to you, what's most important, and what you need in order to fully understand and communicate information.

Shortly after *The Way They Learn* was released, a junior high school in the state of Washington received some grant money for a project to help its Learning Assistance Program (LAP). Although the students in this program were all struggling in school, they weren't eligible for special education funds or instruction. Many of these seventh, eighth, and ninth graders were failing numerous academic subjects, and several were bordering on juvenile delinquency. One teacher, Mrs. Troy,* had chosen to become a full-time instructional aide in order to work with these particular kids. She was also completing her certification as a learning styles specialist. Together we sat down and designed a program that would enable the LAP students to discover and use their learning style strengths to improve their performance in school, as well as to boost confidence in their ability to succeed in life. The school purchased a copy of *The Way They Learn* for each student in the program,

---

*Names have been changed.

and Mrs. Troy was able to use both formal (research-validated) and informal (abbreviated, nonscientific) instruments for assessing the students.

Mrs. Troy was tireless in her efforts, and she single-handedly spent six weeks assessing each of the more than 80 students, helping them pinpoint their dominant learning style strengths in all five of the research models used in the book. I conducted several hours' worth of instruction for the school staff and spoke to interested parents at a PTA program.

The response of the students was overwhelmingly positive. They were flattered that an adult would even *ask* about how they learn. They couldn't imagine that a teacher would actually *want* to develop alternative strategies for studying and learning. Although there were many success stories, one of my favorites is about Jake, a ninth grader who had one foot in the principal's office and the other foot in Juvenile Hall.

Mrs. Troy was determined to get to Jake. He was failing every subject and hadn't done any homework for almost a year and a half. "He's a great kid," insisted Mrs. Troy. "He's bright and capable, and he has a wonderful sense of humor. These grades do *not* reflect what Jake can do." After determining Jake's dominant learning styles, she set up a conference with him.

At first, Jake appeared disinterested in the results of his learning styles assessments. Mrs. Troy picked up a copy of *The Way They Learn* and pushed it across the desk to him.

"This is your book, Jake," she said.

He grinned and shook his head. "Oh no, Mrs. Troy. I don't *read* books."

She persisted. "The book is yours. I'd like you to just look through it," she said.

He shrugged, picked up the book, and walked out.

A few days later, Mrs. Troy received an urgent message in her mailbox in the faculty room. Jake's mother wanted to talk to her right away. With some reluctance and a certain amount of dread, Mrs. Troy called. Jake's mother insisted she come and have a conference in person, so Mrs. Troy arranged to meet with her that afternoon.

Jake's mom was almost breathless when she met with Mrs. Troy. She started talking right away. "I don't know what you've done to my son," she began. "The other day he came home with this book." She held up Jake's copy of *The Way They Learn*. "He said, 'Mom, you've got to read this book! This is *me* in this book!' Then he made his father and me sit down at the kitchen table while he went through all the various learning style descriptions you talked to him about. He kept pointing out the ones that fit him. I've never seen him so excited about something he did at school."

Mrs. Troy smiled, but before she could speak, Jake's mom said, "Here's the best part. Yesterday we were all going to go shopping for school supplies, and Jake asked if we would wait for him while he did his English homework. I almost fainted! We waited, and he finished every bit of homework for the first time in *months!*" She leaned closer, and Mrs. Troy could see her eyes brimming with tears. "I don't know what you've done, but my son is a different boy. Tell me how to make this last!"

Mrs. Troy was able to help Jake's mom, along with dozens of other parents, develop practical strategies to work with their children's learning style strengths. There are plans to continue and expand this program every year for all the students in the school, since many of them begged to be tested for learning styles even though they weren't in the program. The students are excited about the possibilities.

Learning styles is certainly not a magic formula or quick answer to all our problems. But it provides an invaluable framework that can enable us as parents and educators to focus on individual strengths and begin to build confidence within our children for becoming successful, lifelong learners. With our knowledge of learning styles, we can provide parents and teachers with a more detailed road map than we currently distribute through standard school systems. We need to keep finding *many* ways to help our children be successful, and the strategies in the following chapters will give you lots of fuel for the journey.

You will find that this book, while it offers invaluable advice and diverse strategies, holds true to the concept of accountability and high standards of conduct. I do not endorse letting children rely on their learning styles as an excuse, or using their "style" to get away with inappropriate behaviors.

Many adults have grown up feeling that they are not really as smart as everyone else. More and more children are finding that they just don't fit into the traditional education system. Because of our research in learning styles, we have discovered and documented that there are *many* ways of being smart. Each of us was created as a unique and gifted individual. Even those born with severe physical limitations have been endowed with some wonderful gifts and abilities. What a relief it has been for literally thousands of people of all ages to discover that they really do possess capabilities and areas of strength.

As you read this book, you will find that most of what you discover will be helpful for you in understanding *yourself* as well as your children. Keep an open mind as you read, and try to be as flexible as possible when it comes to helping your children succeed by using their learning style strengths. I believe you'll be amazed at the difference your knowledge and use of learning styles will make, both within your own family and among your colleagues at work. You may even discover that the things about your children that frustrate you most are actually some of their greatest strengths and abilities.

Plan of Action

Keep a brief journal of your interactions with and observations of each of your children. If you don't want to make entries daily, do so weekly. Use the following questions as guidelines.

1. What made_____(child's name) happiest this week?

2. What frustrated him/her?

3. What conversation between the two of us this week stands out in my mind? Why?

4. What new approach have I tried with _____this week? How did it work?

5. Which of _____'s strengths really stood out this week?

6. What do I know about_____that I didn't know a week ago?

Chapter Two

Parents, Do *Your* Homework First!

You're probably reading this book because you want to find
ways to help your children be happy and successful. You want
them to achieve in school and become lifelong learners. Before you can help
your children, however, you need to understand your own learning style
strengths. That's where this chapter's assignment comes in—perhaps the most
important homework you *or* your child will ever do.

The following account from Max Lucado's *In the Eye of the Storm* illus-
trates the importance of parents doing their *own* homework before expecting
their children to complete their assignments.

> February 15, 1921. New York City. The operating room of
> the Kane Summit Hospital. A doctor is performing an appen-
> dectomy.
>
> In many ways, the events leading to the surgery are unevent-

11

ful. The patient has complained of severe abdominal pain. The diagnosis is clear: an inflamed appendix. Dr. Evan O'Neill Kane is performing the surgery. In his distinguished thirty-seven-year medical career, he has performed nearly four thousand appendectomies, so this surgery will be uneventful in all ways except two.

The first novelty of this operation? The use of local anesthesia in major surgery. Dr. Kane is a crusader against the hazards of general anesthesia. He contends that a local application is far safer. Many of his colleagues agree with him in principle, but in order for them to agree in practice, they will have to see the theory applied.

Dr. Kane searches for a volunteer, a patient who is willing to undergo surgery while under local anesthesia. A volunteer is not easily found. Many are squeamish at the thought of being awake during their own surgery. Others are fearful that the anesthesia might wear off too soon.

Eventually, however, Dr. Kane finds a candidate. On Tuesday morning, February 15, the historic operation occurs.

The patient is prepped and wheeled into the operating room. A local anesthetic is applied. As he has done thousands of times, Dr. Kane dissects the superficial tissues and locates the appendix. He skillfully excises it and concludes the surgery. During the procedure, the patient complains of only minor discomfort.

The volunteer is taken into post-op, then placed in a hospital ward. He recovers quickly and is dismissed two days later.

Dr. Kane had proven his theory. Thanks to the willingness of a brave volunteer, Kane demonstrated that local anesthesia was a viable, and even preferable, alternative.

But I said there were two facts that made the surgery unique. I've told you the first: the use of local anesthesia. The second is the patient. The courageous candidate for the surgery by Dr. Kane was Dr. Kane.

To prove his point, Dr. Kane operated on himself!

A wise move. The doctor became a patient in order to convince the patient to trust the doctor.[1]

The lesson to be drawn from the preceding story is that before you can pinpoint your children's strengths and preferences, you first must know and understand your own. For one thing, it'll give you insight into why you and your children experience many of the conflicts you do. Also, the way you perceive and deal with information will largely determine the expectations you have for your children. Finally, and perhaps most important, as your children see the difference understanding learning styles makes in *your* life, it will be natural for them to follow your example.

In the next few pages, you'll find a brief review of the five different learning styles models I first introduced in *The Way They Learn*.[2] As you work your way through the descriptions, try to identify your own strengths and preferences. You'll find that you won't fit neatly into any one category and that there are no all-or-nothing methods of recognizing particular learning styles. As you proceed with the general learning styles profile, you'll also be able to consider the strengths of each of your children. Bear in mind that this is not a formal assessment; it is simply a quick and painless way to begin using learning styles to design effective strategies for helping your children be successful, happy, and productive.

GENERAL LEARNING STYLES PROFILE

Environmental Preferences (How Do You Concentrate?)

Researchers Kenneth and Rita Dunn have provided us with hundreds of studies showing how important it is to recognize and use natural learning style strengths when it comes to where, when, and how we study and learn effectively.[3] Not all of the following elements will have the same importance to you, but you'll find them helpful in identifying what kind of environment you need to concentrate best.

Time of Day

After decades of various research projects, scientists have confirmed what most of us have known all along: Each of us has certain times of the day or night when we simply can't be at our best. That doesn't mean we don't learn to cope, but it *does* give us important information about ourselves when it becomes essential that we *really* concentrate.

Think about the time of day when you are naturally more productive. Are you an early morning person or a night owl? Are there consistent times during the day when you find your mind drifting? Have you learned to avoid doing your most difficult tasks at your least effective time of day?

Each child will also exhibit some of these preferences early in life. One will wake up at the crack of dawn, while the other has to be dragged out of bed. One will be dozing on the couch by 6:00 P.M., while the other will be climbing the walls. What we often don't realize is that we can help our children use their time most productively by working *with* their internal clocks instead of against them. For example, I've always been a morning person. The *worst* time for me to do my homework was in the evening. Even now I'm usually better off getting up early (often hard to do, even for the morning person!) and doing my most difficult tasks while I'm fresh and enthusiastic about my day. My husband, on the other hand, can really produce results doing tasks between 9:00 P.M. and 2:00 A.M. and is pretty worthless until about 10:00 A.M. the next day. Naturally, we seem to have produced a son in each category!

Where would you put the mark that indicates *your* best time of day?

Early Bird　　　　　　　　　　　　　　　　　　　　　　　　Night Owl

Intake

I discovered long ago that I almost never got my best work done unless I had something to eat and/or drink while I was concentrating. As an adult, I usually have a cup of coffee handy, as well as a healthy snack for nibbling. When it comes to our children, however, we often don't take into account their need for nutritional intake while they're doing homework or trying to pay attention in class. Although it's not always possible to let your children eat or drink while they're studying, you may be surprised at the increase in learning that takes place when you don't make eating or drinking an issue.

How would you rate your own need for intake?

Eat or Drink to Think　　　　　　　　　　Can't Think While Eating or Drinking

Light

As you're reading this book, what kind of light are you using? If you're one who needs a brightly lit room or study space, chances are good that you insist your children do the same. If you prefer softer illumination, you may actually cringe when you walk into a room flooded with light. As long as a person can comfortably see, there *is* no standard level of light that is necessary for everyone.

Which level of light is comfortable for you?

___

Bright   Soft or Dim

Design

Have you ever walked into your child's bedroom expecting to find her studiously doing her homework at that student desk you paid good money for, only to find both her and her books and papers spread over the bed and floor? Does your child prefer draping over the chair in the living room to sitting quietly at the kitchen table? When it comes to the design of the room or study area, individual preferences are almost always unique. If you prefer to sit at a desk, you can usually expect to have at least one child who prefers the opposite. The question is, does the work get done?

What design do you find yourself gravitating toward when you really have to study or concentrate?

___

Formal (desk, chair, etc.)   Informal (couch, floor, etc.)

Temperature

It's no coincidence that dual controls on electric blankets are more popular than single controls. Although most of us can adapt to various climates when necessary, we usually have a particular temperature range at which we work best. For many children, temperature may not be that important. But for those who can't concentrate unless the room feels comfortable, this may be a more critical issue than you thought.

What about you? What should the temperature be for you to work at your best?

___

Cold   Hot

Modalities (How Do You Remember?)

Modalities is the word we use to describe the various modes of remembering. According to the Walter Barbe–Raymond Swassing model, when you need to remember information, you use at least three basic modes: auditory (hearing), visual (seeing), and kinesthetic (moving).[4] Although each of us uses all three, we often benefit most when we're employing our strongest method.

Auditory

When you need to think, does it help to talk through your thought process? Do you frequently find yourself talking aloud even when no one else is in the room? If your auditory mode is strongest, you need to actually hear yourself *say* what you need to remember. When you are helping your child study, a more auditory learner may really thrive with verbal drill and repetition. Interestingly, strong auditory people, more than others, may need silence while working or concentrating because of how easily other noises distract them.

How strong are your auditory preferences?

_____

Most Preferred   Least Preferred

Visual

Have you ever been listening to someone speak and suddenly found yourself struggling to picture what in the world they're talking about? You may be accused of daydreaming or tuning out when what you were really doing was trying to get a visual handle on the information you need to remember. When you use your visual modality, you will usually find yourself highlighting as you read, or color coding notebooks or files. A strongly visual child is almost always helped by visual aids such as flash cards, pictures, and charts.

When you're dealing with an extremely visual person, you can talk until you're blue in the face and simply be met with a blank stare—until you illustrate what you're saying!

How visual are you?

_____

Very Visual   Not Visual

Kinesthetic

Have you ever been accused of being restless? Do you work best in short spurts? Is some part of your body in almost constant motion? If you answered yes to any of these questions, the chances are good that you are kinesthetic. Simply put, you need to keep moving in order to focus and concentrate on learning and remembering information. For highly kinesthetic children, school is often torture when they have to sit still without a break for long periods. Kinesthetic children will usually learn more by *not* always having to sit still, because they aren't distracted by the lure to get up and move!

How kinesthetic are you?

Very Kinesthetic   Not Kinesthetic

Cognitive Style (How Do You Interact with Information?)

The Herman Witkin model of learning styles helps us understand fundamental differences in the way each of us takes in and communicates information and how we communicate it to others.[5]

Those who are more *analytic* by nature automatically break down the information coming in so that they can deal with it in smaller, component parts. They can focus easily on specific facts, but they may consider the bigger picture to be irrelevant until all the details are understood.

Those who are more *global* tend to be better at grasping the overall situation, getting the gist of things, and assuming the details will fall into place after establishing the big picture.

Although each of us possesses both analytic and global strengths, our bent toward one over the other is especially noticeable when we study or learn. The analytic learner is often overwhelmed when information isn't given in a logical, step-by-step order with clear, specific directions. Global learners, on the other hand, are more easily frustrated by a detailed explanation or specific method without an overall idea of where they're going.

Where would you place yourself on the continuum?

Definitely Analytic   Definitely Global

Multiple Intelligences (How Do You Show You're Smart?)

The traditionally accepted IQ tests are not necessarily what we expect them to be. For generations, we've been led to believe that our scores on IQ tests are definite indicators of how smart we are and how successful we're going to be. The fact is, there are *many* ways of being smart, and IQ tests measure only a small portion of them. Howard Gardner's research uncovered at least seven different intelligences, many of which cannot be measured by standard IQ tests.[6] Although his Multiple Intelligences model is not specifically related to learning styles, it's an important part of the picture. Let's take a quick look at the various ways we can be brilliant!

Linguistic

Linguistic intelligence measures verbal abilities: reading, writing, speaking, and debating, with particular skills in word games and semantics.

How much linguistic intelligence do you feel you have?

High   Low

Logical-Mathematical

Logical-mathematical intelligence has to do with abilities in numbers, patterns, and logical reasoning. Scientists, mathematicians, and philosophers are typically high in this area of intelligence.

How high is your logical-mathematical intelligence?

High   Low

Spatial

Spatial intelligence is the ability to think in vivid mental pictures, restructuring an image or situation in your mind. It is, by the way, also what helps you "find Waldo" in the popular series of hidden pictures.

How does your spatial intelligence measure on the following scale?

High   Low

Musical

Musical intelligence often shows up best through a person's ability with rhythm and melody, as well as general appreciation for orchestration of sounds and words. You don't have to be a professional musician to possess musical intelligence.

How high is your musical intelligence?

High   Low

Bodily-Kinesthetic

Bodily-kinesthetic intelligence helps a person use his/her body skillfully. This intelligence is especially important for surgeons, actresses, artists, athletes, and so on. Though children with this intelligence often get into trouble at school for their constant, restless movement, it will probably benefit them in their careers.

How high is your bodily-kinesthetic intelligence?

High   Low

Interpersonal

Interpersonal intelligence gives a person the ability to intuitively understand and get along with all kinds of people. Almost a "sixth sense," it's essential for pastors, teachers, counselors, and others who help people through difficult times. If you are strong in this type of intelligence, others are drawn to you as a friend and confidant.

Where would you place yourself on this intelligence scale?

High   Low

Intrapersonal

Intrapersonal intelligence is often expressed best in solitude. This is a natural gift for understanding ourselves, for knowing who we are and why we do the things we do. It's usually exhibited more subtly than other types of intelligence and often is overlooked by the casual observer.

How self-smart are you?

_____

High   Low

Mind Styles™ (How Do You Communicate What You Know?)

One of the most interesting and effective learning styles models comes from the research of Anthony F. Gregorc.[7] In his Mind Styles™ model, Gregorc gives us an organized view of how our minds work. We perceive, or take in information, in two ways: *Concrete*—using our five senses; and *Abstract*—using our intuition and imagination. We also order information and organize our lives in two ways: *Sequential*—in a linear, step-by-step manner; and *Random*—in chunks, with no particular sequence. These two ways of perceiving and ordering give us four learning style combinations. Everyone has and uses all four, but most of us are dominant in at least one or two. (See the chart on p. 22 for a more detailed description of the following learning styles.)

Concrete Sequential (CS)

When you're being Concrete Sequential, you are using your practical, predictable side. You're straightforward and down-to-earth. You're stable, reliable, and often provide the "anchor" for those around you.

How well does this describe you?

_____

Definitely   Definitely Not

Abstract Sequential (AS)

Your Abstract Sequential traits show up best when you're being logical, methodical, and analytic. You take your time when making decisions, and one of your greatest assets is your ability to be objective.

How well does this describe you?

_____

Definitely   Definitely Not

Abstract Random (AR)

The aspects of your style that are Abstract Random are what make you especially sensitive to and effective with people. Your spontaneous and flexible nature draws other people to you. You know intuitively what others need.

How well does this describe you?

Definitely   Definitely Not

Concrete Random (CR)

Your Concrete Random nature makes you curious, adventurous, and quick to act on your hunches. It's what drives you to keep changing, growing, and taking risks.

How well does this describe you?

Definitely   Definitely Not

SO, WHAT AM I?

These descriptions are intended to be a brief introduction and/or review. For more details about each of these models, be sure to read my book *The Way They Learn*. Also, if you would like a quick and informal survey designed to help you talk to your children about identifying their learning styles, see the appendixes at the back of the book. Remember, your learning style strengths are pieces of a puzzle, not a neat category you can identify and fit into. You'll discover that recognizing these patterns and preferences will help you communicate more effectively with your children and others around you.

Every parent has an absolutely vital "home" work assignment: *Know your child!* Working your way through this chapter is a giant step toward better understanding your children (and yourself!) by identifying strengths. As you begin to apply this knowledge in the following chapters, keep in mind that each of us possesses unique and wonderful traits and characteristics. Even when yours don't match your child's, you can have a new and profound appreciation for the differences. Didn't you think your homework would be *harder* than this?

Four Combinations

Concrete Sequential (CS)

hardworking

conventional

accurate

stable

dependable

consistent

factual

organized

Abstract Sequential (AS)

analytic

objective

knowledgeable

thorough

structured

logical

deliberate

systematic

Abstract Random (AR)

sensitive

compassionate

perceptive

imaginative

idealistic

sentimental

spontaneous

flexible

Concrete Random (CR)

quick

intuitive

curious

realistic

creative

innovative

instinctive

adventurous

Plan of Action

When it comes to determining learning and personality styles, you'll never fit neatly into any one category. Each of us has many pieces that make up the whole of who we are. The following illustration uses puzzle pieces to show how complex and varied we all are. Our learning style strengths provide an important framework, or border, to the puzzle. If you can, draw a quick diagram of your own personal puzzle.

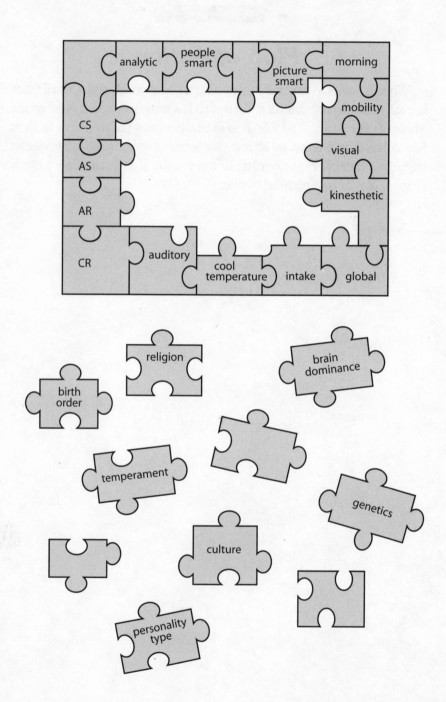

Chapter Three

Moving Them from Excuses to Accountability

"I'm a random—I don't do math."

"I'm a global—I don't *have* to have a clean room."

"I'm a kinesthetic learner—I *can't* sit still."

"I'm a sequential —I don't have to be flexible."

You've probably already heard enough excuses from your children to last a lifetime. So, what if helping your child discover learning styles creates a whole *new* set of excuses? Don't worry. Incorporating learning styles into your approach as a parent or teacher should never take the place of accountability. You don't have to sacrifice academic excellence or lower standards of behavior in order to accommodate a child's learning style strengths. But I do believe it's essential that we focus on what it is we want to accomplish in asking our children to do something. In other words, *what's the point?*

Remember that your *own* personal learning style will greatly influence how you perceive the learning styles of others, especially your children. For example, if you're sequential, your more random children may drive you crazy by their lack of organization. Are they giving you excuses because they don't want to do what you're asking, or do they simply need to find a way to accomplish the goal that makes sense to their styles? How can you tell the difference? I'd like to give you a few ideas about how you can hold your children accountable while still honoring individual learning strengths.

HOLDING YOUR CHILDREN ACCOUNTABLE

1. Define what needs to be accomplished or taught, and then find as many ways as possible to work with your child's learning style so he/she can master it. I remember listening to a local humorist a few years ago when he told about helping his daughter do homework. "I've finally figured out why I had to learn to multiply and divide fractions when I was in the fourth grade," he said. "It was so I could help my fourth-grade daughter do *her* homework!"

Some of the greatest battles fought in the home are over doing homework. Even the brightest and most cooperative kids often struggle with the discipline of this nightly ritual. Perhaps some of the best excuses ever heard have come from kids trying to get out of doing homework. As a teacher, I found I had to ask myself an important question: Why am I giving them these assignments?

Teachers and home-school parents may find the principle of clarifying the point of a task especially helpful in making instruction more effective. For years such things as multiplication tables, long division, sentence diagramming, and other fundamental methods of education have given children fits when they tried to master a vaguely defined concept. Why do you have to memorize multiplication tables? You do need to understand the concept of multiplication, but does everyone benefit from the same approach? Of course not. What's the point? If the point is to understand the mathematical concept in your head, then define your objective and meet it. If the point is that you should know how to do multiplication the long way in case you don't have a calculator handy, then be clear about what it is you're really trying to teach.

If you understand why you need to know what you're teaching your children, you can probably come up with alternative ways to teach the concept that are more compatible with their learning styles.

In *The Way They Learn*, I introduced my readers to a bright, young student named Sarah, who was failing math because she refused to do the homework.[1] Sarah was bored with the work, she said, because she hated doing 20 problems when she understood the concept after doing just three. Even though homework assignments counted for a third of Sarah's total grade, she decided it just wasn't worth it.

Fortunately, in Sarah's case, her teacher was extremely cooperative and open-minded, and he and Sarah struck a deal. Sarah agreed to do at least half of her math homework every night. If she got 92 percent or better on her math test, her teacher would give her full credit for all the lessons. If she got lower than 92 percent, she agreed to complete whichever assignments her teacher deemed necessary.

Sarah kept her end of the bargain. Some nights she did *more* than half of the homework, because now she knew she was doing only what was necessary for her to do well on the test. She never did fall below a 92 percentile on any math test the rest of the year.

Sarah's teacher caused a bit of a stir among the staff at the school. Questions came hard and fast: What if all the children wanted to try this approach? How in the world would you keep track of the various assignments? How would you be sure that every student was being treated equally?

You see, Sarah's teacher had asked himself the important question: What's the point? Since the point of doing the homework was to help his students understand the math concepts, he backed off from the standard requirement of completing every problem on the exercise sheet and began to help both himself *and* his students focus on why the homework was important. Granted, this approach took more time. He also found, however, that he was able to individualize many of his assignments with much less effort than he'd thought possible.

As parents and educators, we must take a good, hard look at why we assign homework. This issue is too important to simply keep using the task as a traditional form of discipline and study. Have we really done a good job of communicating with our students or children the purpose of what we assign?

Many students will complete the assignments simply because it fulfills a grade requirement. But what about the growing number of students who aren't motivated to do homework at all? For teachers and home-school parents especially, I would ask you to do this: If you believe in the importance of what you assign, either challenge yourself to prove to your students that the homework is doing them some good, or challenge the students to prove to you that they don't need to do the homework at all. For those students who recognize the purpose in the work but still believe it's too boring, challenge them to come up with alternative methods of achieving the goal. After all, they have a responsibility for meeting that outcome.

2. Treating people equally does not mean treating them the same.
"Hey, Mom! Charlie's changing everything around—that's not fair!"
"Well, do *you* want to do that?"
"No way! I just don't think it's fair that *he* gets to do it!"

Almost every parent who has more than one child struggles with issues of sibling rivalry, but utilizing each child's unique learning style may alleviate feelings of favoritism or unfairness. Since each of us is an individual, no single teaching method can be effective for everyone. My husband is my opposite in almost every area. If you were to insist that we both be taught in the *same* way when it comes to learning, one of us would be receiving very *unequal* treatment.

As you try to come up with compelling reasons for your children to do what they're told and not worry about their brothers or sisters, keep in mind *the bottom line*. "Look, Tim, the bottom line is this: You get to it one way; your brother gets to it another. The point is, you both accomplish the goal." It's important to teach your children as early as possible to honor the differences between them. If you effectively define the bottom-line outcomes, you'll be more effective in convincing them why treating everyone fairly means they aren't all treated exactly alike.

The traditional school system struggles with this concept because it takes much more time and effort to vary the methods for teaching objectives that often aren't clearly defined in the first place. It's simpler to just quantify everything and measure results by way of objective tests. If we continue to do this, we'll subject many of our children to an educational system that is more like a prison sentence than preparation for a successful, fulfilling life. There are no simple answers to this problem, but there is a simple question: What's the point?

3. Stretching makes us stronger. I remember as a child hearing my mother repeatedly say, "Well, I do a lot of things I don't feel like doing!" I would give her a puzzled look and say, "Why?" Most of us would prefer to do only what is convenient or comfortable for us, but it doesn't take long to figure out that the rest of the world is not particularly anxious to cater to us. In fact, everyone who succeeds at work, school, and home *must* do things they don't like.

If the purpose of our children's education—both at home and at school—is to equip them to deal with life, then some of the most important lessons may be those that stretch them beyond their natural strengths and abilities and challenge them to think or learn in a different way. I believe the key lies in helping a child realize he/she is stretching on purpose. If we don't explain why something may be difficult for them, some children may just assume they're inadequate and so not even *try* to accomplish the task. If, on the other hand, they know where their strengths lie and as a result know what causes them frustration, they can start from a position of confidence and *deliberately* stretch out of what's comfortable.

As a classroom teacher, I often found that if I prefaced tasks with an explanation of what I was asking, my students were more successful. For example, I would say: "Now, this is going to seem a little vague and confusing for you sequentials who need a step-by-step explanation, but stick with me. I'm going to show you where the steps come in." I could see visible relief on the faces of those dominantly sequential students. *Whew!* they would say to themselves. *At least she knows this drives me crazy!* And usually it didn't bother them as much as they thought it would.

HOW MUCH IS A MATTER OF STYLE?

Parents shouldn't use *their* style as an excuse either. Often when we hear ourselves reply "Because I *said* so!" we're really insisting our children do it our way because it's more convenient than trying to figure out how to accomplish the same goal a different way. Other times, it's simply necessary that our children stretch out of what's comfortable for them and learn the discipline of doing what needs to be done.

When you experience conflict with your children, try to keep a perspective that allows you to decide how much of their behavior is due to a difference between your learning styles and how much is due to another cause (emotional, physical, etc.). Most of the time, neither parents nor children set about to deliberately annoy and frustrate each other. We do, however, feel most comfortable when other people do things in a way that makes sense to us, and that's where a knowledge and appreciation of learning styles is going to make a tremendous difference!

The chart on the following pages will help you identify some of the most common excuses used and give you some ideas for moving your children beyond them. As you read through the information, decide how you can hold your children accountable while still being true to their individual learning styles. When you're trying to decide whether or not your children are simply using excuses to avoid doing tasks, ask one important question: What's the point?

Excuses, Excuses!

What's Your Excuse?	Who Usually Gives It, and Why?	How Do We Move Them Beyond It?
"I'm too bored!"	*Concrete Randoms* *(let's-just-get-this-over-with, how-much-is-necessary kids)*	
	They need compelling reasons to learn or pay attention.	If you or their teacher can't make things interesting for them, challenge them to learn how to motivate themselves.
	Analytics/ Abstract Sequentials (how-do-you-know-this, what-makes-you-the-expert kids)	
	They may have lost respect for your credibility or authority.	Establish credibility early on, and make sure they know where the facts come from.
	The task may be too easy to be challenging.	Let them do some of the research and documentation; be sure to recognize their efforts and input.
"The teacher doesn't like me!"	*Abstract Randoms/ Globals (why-can't-everyone-just-get-along, we're-people-too kids)*	
	School and learning must be an intensely personal experience in order to have a lasting effect.	Work on noticing something positive about them as many times as possible during the day.
		When they work with a teacher who may be more analytic or sequential, help the students understand that just because the teacher forgets to be more global or random doesn't mean the teacher doesn't like them.

Excuses, Excuses!

What's Your Excuse?	Who Usually Gives It, and Why?	How Do We Move Them Beyond It?
"I left my books at school!"	*Globals/Randoms* *(out-of-sight-out-of-mind, I-meant-to-bring-it-home kids)* They had too many things to think about at the end of the school day.	Consider buying a second set of textbooks and leaving one set at home and one at school. Set a specific time and/or place each school day where they get together with a partner and quickly list what they need to take home.
"I never have time to finish my assignments!"	*Analytics/ Abstract Sequentials* *(if-there's-not-time-to-do-it-right-I-won't-do-it-at-all, why-are-you-in-such-a-hurry kids)* They need to work through an assignment thoroughly; they need to have clear and specific directions.	Be sure they understand the purpose of the assignment, as well as the reason for the stated deadline. If they need more time, give it to them, as long as you know they are truly working as well as they can. Help them get a "jump start" so they will not agonize over how to begin the assignment.

Excuses, Excuses!

What's Your Excuse?	Who Usually Gives It, and Why?	How Do We Move Them Beyond It?
"I just can't do my math!"	**Globals** *(just-get-the-gist-of-it, what's-the-big-deal kids)* They view math concepts as often overwhelming and rarely personal.	Help them break the concept down into manageable and understandable pieces; break down the assignment whenever possible. Use as many personal examples as possible.
	Randoms *(why-do-I-have-to-follow-the-steps, what's-the-point-anyway kids)* It's often impossible to show their work because they honestly don't know how they got the answer.	Help them apply the math problems in as many situations as possible instead of insisting on a step-by-step sequence, thereby demonstrating they understand the concept.
"I can't concentrate!"	**Analytics/Sequentials** *(give-it-to-me-one-at-a-time, just-stick-to-the-point kids)* They need to focus on one thing at a time and usually can't concentrate while others are talking or interrupting.	Help them keep their work space clutter-free; challenge them to practice working with distractions on less important assignments. Keep household interruptions to a minimum.
	Globals/Randoms *(hey-what's-everybody-doing, how-soon-do-we-do-something-else kids)* They are easily distracted by interesting activities or conversations.	Let them choose a more analytic/ sequential partner who will gently help them keep focused.

Plan of Action

Which excuses do you hear most in your household? Can you think of reasons these excuses are given? What can you do this week to help your child move beyond them?

Chapter Four

What's It Going to Take to Motivate?

She was a bright and capable teenager who had just flunked out of math for the third time. I asked her the question her frustrated parents were desperate to know: "Why did you fail math *this* time?"

She shrugged and smiled grimly. "Because my parents told me 'No way are you going to flunk math again this semester.'"

Obviously, this method of motivating her had *not* had the desired effect!

What do you do when you know your child is achieving far below his/her potential? How do you motivate a procrastinator to start and finish a task? How can you get your children to do what they're told without constantly raising your voice or issuing threats? As you probably know, there are no simple answers or sure-fire recipes, but you *can* find effective ways to inspire almost every learning style by discovering and appealing to the design of the mind. Remember, it's likely that what motivates *you* will not be as effective with your children. You may have to stretch outside your own perceptions to come up with the right words and methods for your children's unique styles.

Although it is important to understand all the learning styles models, the Gregorc model can best help you to motivate and encourage your children to succeed.[1] Using this model as a foundation, I've asked hundreds of students with various dominant learning styles what really motivates them to do their best, both when it's something they enjoy and when it's something they don't want to do at all. Their answers have been consistent, regardless of age or gender, and you may be surprised at the contrast of their responses. The following comments are representative of the most repeated answers to "What motivates you to do something difficult or boring?"

WHAT MOTIVATES THE DIFFERENT STYLES?

The Dominant Concrete Sequentials—The "Gotta-Have-a-Plan, Just-Say-What-You-Mean, Do-It-by-the-Book" Kids

CSs are nothing if not predictable. They do not like surprises, and they do their best when they know *exactly* what to expect. Their concrete nature makes them practical and hands-on, and their sequential bent keeps them organized and concerned with standards and protocol.

CSs almost always agree that tangible rewards are more motivating than intangible ones. In other words, praise and encouraging words are great, but you need to be specific with your comments (e.g., "I especially like the way you organized your thoughts on paper"), and a job well done should translate to a concrete product (e.g., an award, a grade, money). When it comes to school, CS students claim they are most motivated by knowing that their work will be graded and recorded on permanent school records. Even if an assignment is difficult or boring, you simply need to remind them that it will all count toward the goal at the end, and they'll usually get busy and complete the task.

CSs agree that the way an assignment is first given definitely affects how well they'll complete it. They need clear, specific directions, preferably in writing. The best motivation for them to get started quickly is to see a finished sample that earned the highest grade. CSs also find that being able to break down the assignment into smaller, more manageable parts with distinct and separate deadlines is helpful in giving them continuing proof of accomplishment.

To increase or maintain their level of motivation at home, most CSs agree that it's important to have a checklist written out for their chores and responsibilities. The youngest CSs found it immensely helpful to have a visual chart or checklist, with pictures of what the completed tasks would look like (e.g., a picture of a bed that's made or toys that are put away). Rewards that were motivating ranged from gold stars to small bags of M&Ms or an increase in their allowance.

The CSs also wanted to be clear about what definitely does *not* motivate them. They're quick to point out that they have difficulty dealing with anything vague or general. If you say something like "This house is a mess," it doesn't translate into anything specific enough for CSs to know what you mean. Do you mean you want them to clean it up? What part of it? How soon? What do they get if they do it? Spell out your expectations with as much detail as possible, and the CSs will rarely disappoint you.

The Dominant Abstract Sequentials—The "Let-Me-Think-About-It, Don't-Rush-Me, How-Do-I-Know-This-Is-the-Best-Way" Kids

ASs are dedicated to being as thorough and deliberate as possible in almost everything they do. They usually prefer to take their time, even if it means accepting a penalty for being late.

Since ASs thrive on learning for learning's sake, school does not pose the same motivational problems for them as it does for other students. ASs do not need, and frequently don't want, a lot of frivolous rewards for a job well done. They prefer serious and genuine recognition for their achievements and a higher, more challenging level of work the next time around. They agree that grades are highly motivational, as is the opportunity to excel among their classmates.

At home, ASs will usually participate best when they recognize and appreciate the importance of the goal. They prefer a logical, systematic approach and avoid highly charged, emotional situations. Because of their inherent need to analyze and think through situations, you may have to use more patience in your approach to them, giving them sufficient time to complete each task. When it comes to doing difficult or boring tasks, ASs don't really complain much—they believe they should just do what they have to do and get on with it.

One AS shared that as a teenager, his greatest reward for doing unpleasant chores around the house was his parents' promise of free time when he was finished. Nothing was more precious than having a block of time that was entirely up to him to fill, without the pressure of anyone else's expectations.

ASs are *not* motivated by what they term "cheerleading." They do not appreciate enthusiastic attempts to "pump them up" and get them going. If you try to use any kind of emotional approach, including guilt (e.g., "A child who *really* wanted her mother to be happy would keep her room clean"), you'll usually find ASs unmoved.

The Dominant Abstract Randoms—The "All-for-One-and-One-for-All, Why-Can't-We-All-Just-Get-Along, Let's-Make-Sure-Everyone-Is-Happy" Kids

ARs are not nearly as concerned about facts and details as they are about the *people* involved. Although they're just as smart and capable as any other style, they prefer to not waste their intelligence on anything they don't personally care about or can't apply to their own lives.

ARs are highly motivated by the fact that what they do will please those they most love and respect. At school, most ARs admitted they would work like crazy trying to excel for a teacher who loved them. Since ARs are highly susceptible to guilt, many got high grades because of how it would look to their friends or family if they failed. School is a highly social experience for ARs, so they have to consciously dedicate themselves to completing work that must be done independently. One of the greatest motivations for ARs to get homework assignments done is for them to work together as a group—not necessarily talking to each other about the assignment, but simply being in the same room working toward the same goal.

At home, ARs are often the peacemakers, the buffers between argumentative siblings or frustrated parents. ARs are motivated to do just about anything that will help bring about peace and harmony in the household. The promise of a party, a special event, or a sleep-over at a friend's house is often enough to prompt an AR to do the most difficult or boring task. Anything that can be turned into a social event will hold special appeal.

One mom discovered a unique way to help her AR daughter's study group stay focused on homework without making it seem like such a chore. Once a week, they had a "progressive homework party." Each hour they moved to a different room in the house and had another snack while they studied. Each homework party was scheduled only after the previous one had been deemed a success by the amount and quality of the assignments completed. The ARs actually put pressure on their teachers to give them enough work to last a full evening!

ARs aren't motivated by strict and rigid rules. Although they may obey them out of fear of rejection, they can become silently resentful and the tension may, at some point, lead to a blowup. They don't respond well to someone they perceive is trying to control them. Although you may extract some cooperation by force, ARs will usually find a way to eventually break free.

The Dominant Concrete Randoms—The "Boredom-Is-My-Greatest-Enemy, How-Much-Is-Really-Necessary, I've-Got-a-Great-Idea" Kids

CRs are driven by a need to keep things moving. With quick and usually accurate instincts, CRs rarely spend much time researching or debating options—they just go for it, accepting risks as part of life.

School is often seen as an obstacle for the CRs, a hurdle that must be jumped to finish the race. CRs have a difficult time hiding their boredom, and they rarely have the discipline to sit through a lengthy explanation when they're eager to simply get things over with and move on! If they're absent, CRs are more likely to take a zero on the assignments they missed than to take the time to make up the work. They're rarely motivated to deal with anything that is already in the past; the future is much more appealing. The greatest motivation for excelling in school often comes from working with a teacher who has developed a special relationship with the CR student. CRs agree that they would do the hardest and most boring work in the world if they love and respect the teacher who assigns it.

At home, CRs can often irritate their parents by what appears to be a lack of respect and responsibility. CRs are quick to tell us that it isn't a deliberate move to sabotage the family team; it's just that they don't like to be "bossed around." Most CRs claim they would rather have compelling problems to solve than simply have assigned chores to do.

I recall the story of an exasperated father who got his family together for a conference. "Look," he said, "we've got a problem. None of you wants to do your chores. The house is a mess, the trash isn't getting picked up, the phone messages are getting lost, and there aren't enough clean dishes to get through the next meal. We either have to get our act together or we have to hire a maid." As faces around the table brightened, he added: "If we hire a maid, there'll be a 50 percent cut in allowances, a reduction in groceries, and our vacation to Disneyland is off." Suddenly, his CR recognized a compelling problem. In a matter of minutes, the CR had rallied the troops, and everyone walked away from the table with an assigned task, galvanized by a common goal.

CRs will tell you that they're definitely *not* motivated by rules and requirements. Most CRs don't have trouble with authority; the key is in how the authority is *communicated*. The more you use threats or anger, the more the CR will fail to cooperate with you. Remember, you can't really *make* your child obey. By working with your CR's nature, you'll get greater satisfaction in the end.

HOW DO YOU GET THEM TO MOTIVATE THEMSELVES?

We as parents need to realize that motivating our children doesn't mean simply getting them to want what *we* want. We first need to determine and define the goal, and then motivate our children to achieve it. Suppose I told you I was going to send you to Antarctica and I was going to give you a multitude of creative ways to get there. If you didn't want to *go* to Antarctica, it wouldn't make any difference how imaginative my methods were—you still wouldn't go.

I have had many frustrated parents assert that their children "have to learn to get along with the world." Sometimes I need to gently remind them that the jails are full of people who didn't *have* to get along with the world. Why not help motivate your children to *want* to get along with the world? Then, if they have a strong and positive relationship with their parents, you'll be the ones they turn to for advice on how to do it.

Sometimes the biggest help parents can be to their growing children is to encourage them to discover for themselves what motivates them. After all, when they leave home, there is usually no one who will try to keep them motivated like you did.

One mom tried the self-motivated approach with her son who simply couldn't seem to remember to take the trash out. She sat down with him and asked, "Andy, what do you think would motivate you to take the trash out on time every week?"

Andy shrugged and said, "Nothing. I don't *want* to take the trash out."

Undaunted, Mom told him she wanted him to think about it and she would ask him again in a couple days. Two days later, she repeated her question. "Andy, have you been thinking about what would motivate you to take out the trash?"

He shrugged again, but said, "Money. Cash money."

"How much money are we talking about?"

"Five thousand dollars," Andy said calmly.

Mom resisted the urge to show her first reaction to this absurd reply. She looked him in the eye and echoed his response. "Five thousand dollars?"

Andy grinned. "Okay, five dollars."

Mom thought a minute. "Okay," she said. "For the next three weeks, I'll give you five dollars if the trash is where it's supposed to be when it's supposed to be there. But after that, I want you to tell me something *else* that will motivate you—something other than money. Maybe a special privilege or some free time."

This approach does two things. First, Andy's mom will not fall into the trap of having to pay for every chore she wants Andy to do. Most important, it gets Andy to think about what *would* motivate him. As he grows up, he needs to learn what it takes to get himself to do things he doesn't want to do. When his mom isn't around to spur him on, he'll know how to inspire himself.

Keep in mind that learning styles, in and of themselves, are value neutral—that is, they're neither bad nor good. There's no single best style, nor does any style make a person smarter or more capable than another. People are so complex that labels never fit neatly anyway. So don't worry about which category your child fits into. If one set of motivation strategies doesn't work, try another.

Sometimes you may simply have to retreat and decide what really needs to be an issue. If you help your child develop worthy goals and ambitions, you'll usually find he/she is much more willing to be motivated to achieve them.

The following chart provides specific ideas for motivating the different learning styles, regardless of their age.

Never Too Late To Motivate!

Dominant Concrete Sequentials
(They need PROOF of accomplishment)

If it's EASY, they'll do it because . . .

- the directions are precise and specific
- the outcome is well-defined and realistically achieved
- there is a definite benefit and a tangible reward

If it's HARD, they'll probably do it if . . .

- you can convince them it will make a difference in their grade
- you can explain the project in a step-by-step manner and/or break down the assignment into smaller parts
- you can provide some examples of successful work

Dominant Abstract Sequentials
(They need a SENSE of accomplishment)

If it's EASY, they'll do it because . . .

- it's logical and makes sense
- the goal is well-defined and worthwhile
- it contributes to a general love of learning

If it's HARD, they'll probably do it if . . .

- it comes from a credible source and appears to be reliable
- they are given enough time and advance notice
- they can see where it fits into the greater scheme of things

Never Too Late To Motivate!

Dominant Abstract Randoms
(They need a FEELING of accomplishment)

If it's EASY, they'll do it because . . .

- everyone they like or admire is doing it, too
- it's fun and provides variety and flexibility
- the teacher is someone they really like

If it's HARD, they'll probably do it if . . .

- it will help them feel loved and accepted by parents and peers
- you can convince them it will personally affect their lives for the better
- it's really important to someone they love

Dominant Concrete Randoms
(They need the REWARDS of accomplishment)

If it's EASY, they'll do it because . . .

- there's a sense of adventure—something to be conquered
- it's compelling, fast-moving, and intriguing
- they can treat it lightheartedly and with a sense of humor

If it's HARD, they'll probably do it if . . .

- they are convinced it can get them where they want to go
- they are doing it for someone who really loves and appreciates them
- they can hit the high points and then move on

Plan of Action

Fill out a separate sheet of paper for each child, and answer the following questions:

1. What is_____(child's name) most motivated by?
2. What is_____least motivated by?

Now ask each child (providing he/she is old enough) to answer the same questions. Compare your answers and discuss.

Chapter Five

Turning Conflict into Cooperation

"It's not my *turn* to clean up the kitchen!"

"Mom, make him stop *looking* at me like that!"

"But Dad said I *could!*"

"She *always* gets the best jobs!"

Do any of these statements sound familiar? If your household is not as peaceful and harmonious as you'd like it to be, maybe everyone at home could use a little practice in appreciating each other's learning style strengths. It's ironic that we seem to be drawn to people who possess the traits and characteristics that we lack. When I married my husband, who is totally opposite from me in style, I thought I was simply getting a refreshingly different perspective. I quickly realized it wasn't so refreshing when I had to translate much of what I said into a language his learning style could understand. Working through our differences has helped us realize that the strengths each of us brought to the relationship could combine to make us a strong team.

However, just about the time we began to get a handle on how each of *us* processed information, along came our two sons, each bringing with him a whole new set of communication challenges!

In this chapter, I'd like to give you some ideas on how to turn family conflict into cooperation. First we're going to look at the strengths each dominant learning style can bring to the family when we focus on the positive aspects of individual differences. Then, armed with this knowledge, we'll see how we can apply what we've learned to smooth potential trouble spots in our family relationships. Remember, none of us possesses a pure learning style, but we can all admit to having definite bents and patterns of learning.

WHAT EACH STYLE CAN CONTRIBUTE TO THE FAMILY

Auditory

You can spot the auditory learners by their need to talk. Their strength lies in their ability to work through a thought process verbally, using trusted friends or family members as sounding boards. You don't usually have to wonder what an auditory person is thinking—just listen and you'll know!

Visual

The visual learners are good at capturing a verbal concept by using a vivid picture or chart. If you're having a hard time imagining how something will look, often the visual family member can bring the idea to life on paper for you.

Kinesthetic

These learners have a high degree of energy, which can be a plus when you've run out of steam. Take advantage of the restless and animated spirit of the kinesthetic family member by letting him/her run the errands, chase the dreams, and keep everyone moving.

Analytic

Analytics can look at the big picture and break it down into manageable parts. Their natural ability to bring order out of chaos can be invaluable. In overwhelming situations when you aren't sure where to begin, the analytic family member can help you identify a good starting point.

Globals

Globals are better than most at grasping an overall concept and then translating it into terms almost everyone can understand. They're also great at figuring out how small pieces fit into a big picture.

Concrete Sequentials

CSs are strong in organization and detail, and they can quickly figure out how much time a project will actually take. Another of their gifts is the ability to take someone's great idea and turn it into a practical, concrete product.

Abstract Sequentials

ASs can be a wonderful resource for checking and documenting information. ASs will take the time and effort to research and evaluate information and make sure that the facts are right, the values are genuine, and the sources are credible.

Abstract Randoms

ARs have an intuitive sense of others' needs and feelings, and they are gifted peacemakers. They often provide the glue that keeps the family together, constantly searching for ways to keep everyone happy. ARs will also provide spontaneity and flexibility, even in the most difficult circumstances.

Concrete Randoms

CRs will always keep things interesting. They are visionaries who dare to dream the impossible. They can inspire, motivate, and energize the rest of the family. The CR family member will make sure no one stagnates or loses momentum, constantly pushing the envelope toward new adventures.

HOW UNDERSTANDING EACH STYLE
CAN REDUCE FAMILY CONFLICT

Acknowledging the individual learning styles within your family is the first step toward bringing everyone together as a team. The next step is *understanding* how these various styles manifest themselves, because only then will you be able to depersonalize conflict every time it crops up.

During a recent seminar series, a grateful mom told me how understanding learning styles had brought her family closer together. Her husband is a career military officer and a dominant Concrete Sequential. His strict and rigid approach to dealing with his dominantly Concrete Random, global teenage daughter, Amy, created almost unbearable friction between them. Then Amy took a two-week learning styles course through her school and began eagerly relating her experiences to her parents. Their curiosity piqued, Mom and Dad attended one of my seminar series to see what the concept was all about. Shortly after, Dad came home one evening to find that Amy had not completed the tasks he'd left for her. As he launched into a stern and detailed lecture, Amy interrupted him. "Oh, Dad—you're being so *CS!*" To Mom's amazement, Dad began to smile, and soon both he and Amy were laughing. With the tension broken, father and daughter began to negotiate deadlines for the assigned tasks.

Often just referring to what you need in less personal terms can make a big difference in how you and your children relate to, and cooperate with, each other. Saying "I need you to be real sequential for a few minutes" sounds a lot nicer than "Do you think you could *focus* for a few minutes?" The bottom-line accountability doesn't need to change at all—just the method for helping your children achieve it.

WHEN PARENTS HAVE DIFFERENT LEARNING STYLES

Chances are good that in every family where there are two parents, there will be two different learning styles. Although the potential for great teamwork exists, there's also room for conflict between parenting styles. The analytic parent may emphasize the importance of maintaining a consistent code of conduct, while the global parent insists there needs to be room for exceptions. The sequential parent may dictate a predictable routine, while the random counterpart has difficulty even remembering what the routine is supposed to *be*. Since these parents probably have children with different learning styles, how can they present a unified front? How can they agree on parenting strategies for their children when they may not even agree on what's most important between the two of them?

Parents of opposite styles must make a concentrated effort not to work against each other's style. Identify the outcomes and goals you want to set for your family before you discuss the methods you think are needed for achieving them. Once you have agreed on those bottom-line outcomes, recognize that each of you may have different approaches. As long as you're both committed to the objective, give yourselves room for compromise. As soon as your children are old enough, enlist their help in establishing basic family policies. Then talk about some of the various ways to reach the same destination, emphasizing the importance of the bottom line.

If you're a single parent, it's even more critical for your children to recognize and appreciate learning style differences. When your children realize that you're not *deliberately* trying to frustrate and annoy them, they may also understand that the way they're using their styles is making life more difficult for you. Though all of you may become exhausted in your efforts to make the team work, you'll find that your energies are well rewarded when you recognize how valuable you are to each other.

FOCUSING ON THE BEST

The following charts provide examples of how you can make the most of individual family learning style strengths while working toward a common goal during two stressful times of the year: the holidays and summer. Remember, cooperation means that everyone recognizes and appreciates each other's *strengths*, focusing on the *best* aspects of each person.

Peace on Earth at Home During the Holidays

Don't let the holiday season provide more stress than it does happiness. This year, try to make the most of the gifts God created in each individual. Remember that each family member is unique, and sometimes the best gift of all is understanding.

For Dominant Concrete Sequentials

Quick Review of What They Need:
> *Organization*
> *Predictability*
> *Scheduled routine*
> *Literal communication*
> *Contingency plans (What if?)*
> *A beginning, a middle, and an end*
> *Step-by-step instructions*
> *Tangible rewards*

- Put them in charge of recording everyone's wish list for Christmas gifts. They can help design a form that can be filled out, or they can simply record each person's list on a sheet of paper.
- Let them be in charge of organizing, sorting, and arranging the gifts under the tree. Encourage them to check for loose gift tags or torn paper. When it's time to open the gifts, put them in charge of distribution.
- Give them the ads in the weekend newspaper, and let them find items and/or coupons for the things that appear on each family member's wish list. Provide an envelope for each person's list for appropriate coupons and ads.

For Dominant Abstract Sequentials

Quick Review of What They Need:

> *Lots of time to work through a project*
> *Resource material*
> *Logical, step-by-step instruction*
> *Credible sources of information*
> *Opportunities for analysis*
> *Appreciation for their ideas and advice*

- Put them in charge of finding the best price for items on the family's wish lists. Help them comparison shop through the newspaper ads or through the envelopes that the Concrete Sequential sibling provides.
- Challenge them to figure out how much money it would take to buy everything that everybody wants on his/her list for Christmas.
- Let them come up with some ideas for gift giving for an adopt-a-child or adopt-a-family project. Help them decide which gifts make the most sense, given the parameters (age, needs, etc.).

For Dominant Abstract Randoms

Quick Review of What They Need:

> *A personal reason for doing almost anything*
> *Frequent praise and reassurance of worth*
> *Acceptance and appreciation of personal feelings and "illogical" opinions*
> *An opportunity to work with someone else*
> *A feeling of harmony with virtually everyone*
> *An opportunity to use creativity and imagination*

- Challenge them to help the house look and feel like the real spirit of Christmas. What kind of decorations will we need? How many can we make ourselves?

- Let them select names from the adopt-a-family gift tree and help decide what to buy. Besides the actual gifts for the adopted family, what could we make ourselves that would communicate Christmas love?
- Let them decide how they would like to present the Christmas story before the family celebrates by opening gifts.

For Dominant Concrete Randoms

Quick Review of What They Need:
   Inspiration
   Compelling reasons
   Independence
   Freedom to choose
   Opportunities to provide alternatives
   Guidelines instead of rules

- Challenge them to come up with a new annual family tradition for Christmas. Be specific and firm with parameters (how much it could cost, who it would involve, etc.).
- Let them propose a holiday family outing during Christmas vacation. Give them a budget and guidelines, and challenge them to find the best place to go. (Give them extra credit if they can find coupons or discounts!)
- Encourage them to participate on their own as well as with the family in an adopt-a-child program. Offer to match whatever money they can provide for a gift, and challenge them to "shop till you drop."

For the Kinesthetic, Highly Active Child

Remember: The chances are good that you may not be a kinesthetic, highly active person yourself, so try to understand the need for constant motion.

For younger children: Keep them moving! How about running "errands" such as checking the Christmas lights and reporting which ones are out, or having at least one meal a day that's a "movable feast" (eat each course in a different location).

For older children: Keep them moving! When they come to the store with you, give them a clipboard and a checklist of items to be found in the store. Have them write down the location and price of each item. Maybe have a "mystery item" that you list only by description and price; if they find it, they win a small prize or an extra privilege.

Summer Survival Sheet

"I'm bored—there's nothing to do!"
"This is dumb—why did we have to come here?"
"Mom! She hit me!"
"Make him stop looking at me!"
"Why do we always have to go camping together?"

It's summer, and school's out. Now you get to spend more time with your children. Uh-oh, let's admit it—sometimes spending more time as a family sparks conflict and strife along with the desired togetherness. If you hear any of the above statements coming from *your* children, here are some ideas to help you survive.

For Dominant Concrete Sequentials

(the gotta-have-a-plan, just-say-what-you-mean, do-it-by-the-book kids)

- Put them in charge of the calendar. Buy or make an oversized calendar of the summer months and post it on the kitchen wall. Fill in all the events and activities you have planned, and be sure to designate certain dates as unplanned, spontaneous fun days.
- For the major trips or summer events, let these kids design a checklist for items that will be needed. Encourage them to talk to each family member about what he/she will need and compile individual as well as group checklists to be completed before the trip.
- Ask them to design at least one contingency plan for each major summer event. For example, what happens if it rains and you can't do the outdoor picnic for the family reunion?

For the Dominant Abstract Sequentials

*(the let-me-think-about-it, don't-rush-me,
how-do-I-know-this-is-the-best-way kids)*

- Put them in charge of finding the best price for the items on the checklist made by the Concrete Sequentials for the family trip. Help them comparison shop through newspaper ads or garage sales.
- Challenge them to figure out a family vacation budget for the summer, taking into account major and minor trips and events.
- Prepare them for changes in the calendar with as much advance notice as possible, even if it's only a few minutes. For example, as all of you are getting ready to go roller-skating, don't say, "Hey! I've got a great idea! Let's go swimming instead of skating!" Instead, say, "Hey, what would you think about going swimming instead of skating?" Then let them think about or even briefly discuss the pros and cons for a few minutes before coming to a decision.

For the Dominant Abstract Randoms

*(the all-for-one-one-for-all, why-can't-we-all-just-get-along,
let's-make-everyone-happy kids)*

- Let them be the "social chairperson." Commission them to find out what would make each family member happy. Armed with the calendar and checklists made by siblings, let them interview family members and add a personal touch to each person's checklist.
- Let them plan for the times when having friends over along with the family would be appropriate. Help them distinguish between family times and party times, and give them a lot of input into the party times.
- Let them write in a few days over the summer that are "do-nothing days." These are days when they can actually do absolutely nothing if they feel like it and do so guilt-free.

For the Dominant Concrete Randoms

*(the boredom-is-my-greatest-enemy,
let's-keep-things-moving, I've-got-a-great-idea kids)*

- Challenge them to come up with new adventures for family outings this summer. Be specific and firm with your parameters (cost, distance, etc.) and then let them use their imagination.
- Encourage them to design ways to earn or save money during the summer, especially those kids who are too young to get a formal job. Again, be specific and firm with your parameters, but challenge them to think about ways to make money and cut costs. (For example, give them a percentage of each coupon they find that you actually use.)
- Offer incentives for cooperation during family gatherings and events. For example, if they go on a family event without complaining, they can host their own summer party or outing for a few of their friends.

Don't let the lazy, crazy days of summer provide more stress than happiness. This year, try to make the most of the gifts God created in each individual in your family, and remember to discover and appreciate the way they learn!

Plan of Action

What is your greatest challenge for working together as a family? Try holding a family meeting and deciding on one project you would like to accomplish together. Be sure everyone gives input, and try to assign individual responsibilities that will match each person's learning style strengths.

Chapter Six

Dealing with Issues of Discipline

She looked like such an adorable, little girl.
"Angela!" Her mother sounded exasperated. "Angela, I said get over here *right this minute!*"

I watched the face of this beautiful five-year-old standing in the aisle of the department store suddenly darken with a scowl.

"*No!*" she cried. "I want to go see the toys *now!*"

Her mother looked exhausted as she grabbed Angela's hand and began to drag her, screaming, through the store. As they passed me, I saw the mother's eyes roll upward as she muttered, "Just another ordinary day."

If you're the parent of a strong-willed child, you know how frustrating it can be to see your bright, loving, creative offspring turn suddenly into a stubborn, immovable force. What did you do to deserve such defiance? How can this wonderful kid turn into such a monster?

Frustrated parents all over the world face the challenge of disciplining their

65

children without breaking their spirit. As loving parents, we want to do what's best, but it's often difficult for us to accept and remember that each child is different and unique and responds to some forms of discipline better than others. Though this brings a distinct challenge to the concept and practice of effective discipline, it also assures us that we can maintain bottom-line accountability while we honor each child's style.

Before I outline specific discipline strategies for dealing with each learning style, let me remind you of some essential concepts that can be effective with *all* styles.

ESSENTIAL STRATEGIES FOR ALL LEARNING STYLES

1. Authority and accountability should always stay intact. I was one of those Concrete Random, strong-willed kids, and I can tell you that virtually every child wants to respect authority and expects to be held accountable. An understanding of learning style strengths can actually help you reinforce accountability by communicating your authority in a way that makes the most sense to each child.

2. Remember, you can't force your child to obey. When I became a new mother of twins, I made a startling and frustrating discovery. Although these babies were less than seven pounds each, there were still certain things I simply could not *force* them to do! For example, I couldn't force them to love me or respect me. Like it or not, each of us, no matter how young, has a free will. As parents, we must realize that we cannot force our children to obey simply because we demand that they do.

3. The strength and quality of your relationship with your child has more power than any discipline technique. This concept is closely related to the preceding one. Since we can't force our children to obey us, the better our relationship with them, the more likely they are to respond positively to our guidance. Early in my parenting career, I made a profound discovery regarding my strong-willed child Michael. During the times that he and I aren't "locking horns," I work hard at maintaining a solid and loving relationship with him. As a result, he and I are close. When I am upset with him, he can't stand to have our relationship on such poor terms. As a result, my disciplinary efforts are more effective. If your children don't care that you're upset with them, your efforts at disciplining them will have little impact. If you do have a good, loving relationship with your children, nurture it by exercising your disciplinary power carefully. Children are particularly sensitive to heavy-handedness and injustice, which can cause a good relationship to quickly sour.

4. *Remember to ask yourself, "What's the point?"* Even young children need to know *why* things are important. Our children don't have to *agree* with our reasons, but we do owe them the courtesy of an explanation if they want one. If you find yourself arguing frequently with your child and it has turned into a power struggle, try calmly stating the reason for what you're asking, and then state the consequences for disobedience. If your child continues to disobey, follow through with the consequences. Remember, the action you take will be much more effective than the anger or other emotions you show. If you raise your voice often when disciplining your child, insisting that he/she had better do what you say or else, you may find that you've been tuned out.

With older kids, let them have some input into the situation. Define your parameters and be specific about your goals. Then ask for their ideas when it comes to accomplishing the goals. Be firm and friendly when letting everyone know up front what the consequences for disobedience will be, and make sure you reinforce the entire conversation with love and appreciation for their participation in the process.

ESSENTIAL STRATEGIES FOR INDIVIDUAL LEARNING STYLES

The key to successfully communicating authority and meting out discipline usually lies in *how* you do it. The following strategies can help you accomplish important goals with your children without sacrificing accountability, but also without squelching the natural design of their minds.

For Highly Kinesthetic Children

For these kids, put as much action into your words as possible. With younger children, for example, you may need to actually pick them up and physically remove them from a room. Use bodily movements as much as you can to illustrate what you're saying (e.g., sign language or hand motions). Sometimes you may be able to literally "walk them through" a particular situation.

One exasperated mother had told her active five-year-old son numerous times *not* to rub the cat's fur the wrong way. When the perturbed feline showed up with its hair again standing on end, the mom had had enough. She took her son's hand, held it under her own, and gently but firmly smoothed the cat's fur. After a few seconds of maintaining the rhythm, she removed her hand and was delighted to see her son continue stroking the cat's fur properly.

For Highly Auditory Children

When you lay out rules or discuss consequences, ask your highly auditory child to repeat what you said. Remember that auditory learners often remember best what they can put into a rhyme or song. Since having a sense of humor usually helps immensely, try coming up with some "consequence rhymes"—for example, "Not in time, end of the line!" or "Jump from the chair, nothing new to wear!"

For Highly Visual Children

Often something as simple as a poster or illustrated checklist is enough to drive home a point to your visual child. When I was a child, my parents had a plaque with a doghouse and four removable wooden dogs bearing the names of each family member hanging on hooks outside the doghouse. Whenever any of us (Mom and Dad included) got in trouble for some reason, the dog bearing our name was placed inside the doghouse. To this day, the visual impact of being "in the doghouse" has had a lasting effect!

For Dominantly Analytic Learners

Be as specific as possible when you're disciplining your analytic child or teenager. Dealing with a general situation is too overwhelming—break it down into smaller, more manageable parts. For example, when dealing with the issue of broken curfew, instead of saying "We can't have you breaking curfew, Tom!" say something like "Tom, we need you to be home on weeknights no later than 10:00 P.M. Last night you didn't get in until 10:30."

With your analytic child or teenager, it's important to separate the deed from the doer. The less personal you can make your criticism, the better—for example, "Susan, you must have done this without thinking. I know this doesn't make you look as smart as you are." (Please note that this will *not* work with the more global children—they almost always take *everything* personally!)

For Dominantly Global Learners

For kids with this learning style, always start with an overall statement of love and support before you focus specifically on any wrongdoing. These children need to maintain a general sense of well-being, knowing your love is unconditional and not dependent upon their behavior. For example, "John, I've never loved anyone more than I love you, and it really disappoints me that this happened." Often it's best not to recount specific details of the offense unless you honestly believe your child doesn't understand what he/she did wrong. A more general statement may suffice: "Do you understand why you're in trouble?"

If you yourself are more analytic, it may be difficult to remember how important it is to your global children that you don't immediately tell them exactly what behavior needs to be changed. For globals, the indirect approach is almost always more effective than the frontal attack. For example, instead of saying "Allison, you need to take that trash out right now," you may get a better response from a hint: "Boy, that trash is really beginning to smell bad!" Suddenly, Allison pipes up, "Oh yeah, I've got to take it out now."

For Dominant Concrete Sequentials

For most CSs, when it comes to discipline, consistency goes a long way. Establish certain unchanging rules, and write them down. For the visual CSs, suggest they find pictures to illustrate each rule. Make sure the CSs know what the consequences for disobedience will be, and be sure to follow through in each situation. If you're a dominantly random parent, your best bet will be choosing as few and as simple rules as possible so you won't forget or be tempted to suddenly change your mind.

Help your CSs cope with exceptions to the rules by giving as much notice as possible. For example, "Kelli, I know we don't usually let you stay up after 10:00 P.M., but tomorrow we're going to need to bend that rule a little."

For Dominant Abstract Sequentials

For AR children, justice is an important concept. What's fair for one is fair for all. A dominantly random parent runs the greatest risk of being viewed as weak or inconsistent simply by virtue of wanting to consider mitigating circumstances. Be clear in your expectations and logical in your punishments and consequences. Be sure your AS understands the purpose for a particular rule, and whenever possible, try to allow the AS to have at least some input into the setting of rules in the first place.

Although it's always important to show children how much we love them, too much emotion is often difficult for AS children to handle. For example, the more you are visibly upset or angry, the more likely it will be that your AS will be less responsive and may withdraw completely.

For Dominant Abstract Randoms

For most ARs, the whole process of discipline, criticism, or correction is traumatic. Because harmony is so important, ARs will often need less discipline simply because they try so hard to please their parents and keep peace in the family. When it's necessary to punish your AR child, always surround every word or action with love. You can do this sincerely while still driving home the point. For example, "Sandy, you're very important to me. I can't let you behave like this. Will you help me keep our relationship on good terms?"

Because ARs are so susceptible to guilt, you should make a conscious effort to use it sparingly. Your aim should not be to make ARs feel bad—that will happen automatically. The purpose in your punishment should be to correct a problem and reassure your AR that your love and acceptance remain unchanged.

For Dominant Concrete Randoms

CRs may present the greatest challenge when it comes to discipline. You'll find that traditional methods of punishment often will not work with them. CRs believe that, for the most part, rules are simply *guidelines*, meant to be followed to the letter only if absolutely necessary. If you're a CS parent, you may find yourself frequently confronting your CR child over specific issues in which the CR claims he/she essentially did what you wanted but just didn't do it the *way* you wanted it done. With CRs, it's especially important to answer the question "What's the point?" You'll have greater success in maintaining discipline if you can be more flexible with the methods than with the bottom-line accountability.

Most CRs do not have trouble with authority—they have trouble with how that authority is *communicated*. The best way to explain it is what I call my *drive-through theory*. When I stop at a fast-food drive-through and give my order to the little box, I often hear something like "That will be $3.86. Please drive forward." Isn't that a keen sense of the obvious? Give me a break! Do they think I'm too stupid to know I'm supposed to go to the window? By the time I get up to the cashier, I'm so irritated I never want to come back. On the other hand, when I hear "That will be $3.86 at the first window, please," I know exactly what I'm supposed to pay and exactly where I'm supposed to go. But it's said in a way that assumes I'm a smart and capable person. Now that may not seem like a big deal to a lot of people, but to us CRs, it's essential that we're given a little credit for knowing the right thing to do.

NO QUICK RECIPES

Always remember that each child is a complex and wonderful mixture of learning style strengths—and that there's a little bit of all styles in every one of us! When it's necessary to discipline a child, it's usually stressful at best. Don't worry about memorizing specific techniques or labels. Use some variety and flexibility in your strategies, constantly monitoring and adjusting to find what really works.

You may not have to apologize to your children for the outcomes you expect, but you may occasionally need to say you're sorry for forcing them to use only your methods for achieving them.

There is one more important point I'd like to make. Every parent knows there are times when you simply can't negotiate, days when you're too exhausted to strike a bargain, situations that have made you too frustrated to figure out a strategy that will work with your child's learning style. If you're making an honest effort most of the time to use the ideas and strategies that work with each individual child's learning strengths, you'll find that in situations in which you need to just "pull rank" and insist your children obey you because you're the parent and you *said* so, they will be surprisingly more cooperative. If you use this approach sparingly, you'll find it has the power and influence necessary to keep your children responsive to your authority.

The following charts will give you a little more practice in developing a variety of strategies for reaching accountability using the unique design of each child's mind. Even when the discipline dilemma is universal and ageless, you may be surprised to discover how many different reasons there are for bad behaviors and how many effective tactics you can use for solving the problems.

Universal Discipline Problem: Bedtime Battles

Reasons Why   *Things to Try*

Dominant Concrete Sequentials

1. There is no predictability about night-time routines.

2. A change in schedule comes about too abruptly.

3. There are still too many things that need to be done.

1. Establish a bedtime routine and stick to it; post it visually, if it helps.

2. Give at least a two-minute warning before bedtime so they can prepare themselves.

3. At least 30 minutes before bedtime, check with them to see what still needs to be done and how you can help.

Dominant Abstract Sequentials

1. Tasks started are not yet completed.

2. They are not prepared for the next day.

3. There is no sense of closure to the day.

1. Help them prepare early, completing tasks and events to their satisfaction.

2. Arrange clothes and materials for the next day.

3. At least one hour before bedtime, check to see what they feel must be done before bed, and see what you can do to help.

Dominant Abstract Randoms

1. They don't want to disconnect from friends and family.

2. They feel too isolated alone in the bed-room.

3. They don't feel there is anything to look forward to tomorrow.

1. Ask them what will comfort them most—a stuffed animal, a night light, leaving the door open?

2. Establish a personal, close night-time routine—reading a book, a quiet conversation, prayers, etc.

3. Spend a few moments talking about the next day, not from a preparation stand-point but in a way that builds enthusiasm and anticipation.

Reasons Why *Things to Try*

Dominant Concrete Randoms

1. They feel a lack of control.

2. Their energy level is still high.

3. They have too many things on their minds.

---

1. Allow some negotiation on minor points—which bed, what pajamas, which night light, etc.

2. Be sure they have had lots of opportunities to burn up energy well before bedtime, even if you have to make up excuses for running errands, etc.

3. Help them talk through what happened today (but don't press for details!), and talk about what will happen tomorrow.

Universal Discipline Problem: Lack of Respect

Reasons Why   *Things to Try*

Dominant Concrete Sequentials

1. The random parent seems inconsistent or unreliable.

2. They are frustrated because they don't know what's expected of them.

3. They believe everyone should do things their way.

---

1. Establish simple, bottom-line rules you can consistently enforce; be clear about "truth and consequences."

2. Keep them focused on what you need to have them accomplish; be as specific as possible.

3. Point out how many ways there may be to achieve any one goal.

Dominant Abstract Sequentials

1. The parent isn't as systematic and logical as they are.

2. They become impatient with the parent who lacks structure.

3. Their preference to be alone makes them seem aloof or distant.

---

1. State bottom-line accountability and calmly lay out the consequences. Ask "Do you think that's fair?" If they say it's not, press for their reasoning and logically work through the issue.

2. Try to schedule times to explain and discuss expectations. Give them the opportunity for input and limited debate.

3. Try not to take the aloofness personally; give them some time and distance to respond to you.

Reasons Why   *Things to Try*

Dominant Abstract Randoms

1. They are defensive and feel inadequate because they lack strong sequential ordering ability.

2. They succumb to peer pressure—it just seems like the thing to do.

3. They resist what they see as your constant efforts to change "who they are."

1. Be sure they understand that your discipline doesn't affect your love for them.

2. Don't force them to choose between their peers and you—encourage them to see how their actions can influence their friends.

3. Recognize that there may be many ways to achieve a goal—be as flexible as possible right up to the bottom line.

Dominant Concrete Randoms

1. They sense a lack of respect from you in the way that you treat them.

2. They resist doing something just because you said so.

3. They are constantly looking for short cuts and opportunities for negotiation.

1. Don't state the obvious—assume they are intelligent and capable; acknowledge their uniqueness, and enforce the bottom line.

2. Avoid ultimatums and statements beginning with "You must," "You will," "There's no way you're going to . . ."

3. Make the distinction clear between negotiable and nonnegotiable issues; be as flexible as possible.

Plan of Action

Fill out a separate sheet of paper for each of your children. At the top, write down an issue that has often become a discipline problem between you and this child. Divide the paper into two columns; label one side "Reasons Why," and the other, "Things to Try." Then start writing as many things as you can think of in both columns. If your child is old enough, discuss what you've written and ask if he/she agrees with you.

Chapter Seven

What's the Big Deal About School?

Many students are much more intelligent than school has shown them to be. Likewise, many parents have been convinced that there is something wrong with their children when that simply may not be true. Traditional classrooms, inflexible systems of measurement and evaluation, and established methods of instruction don't fit every student. You know your child is bright and capable; you understand that children need to learn discipline and structure, but what happens when your child seems to constantly be at odds with the school system? Do you automatically assume your child is doing something wrong?

Our children spend a significant part of their lives going to school, and their self-esteem reflects, to a great degree, how well they're perceived by educators on their "permanent records." But how much of school should really be such a big deal? How can parents know when their children really lack basic skills as opposed to when their children simply don't fit into a standard mold?

Obviously, there are no simple answers, but I would challenge you to take a serious look at the many different ways of being intelligent. If you can help your children identify their learning style strengths, you can also point out why those same strengths can become obstacles when they encounter various academic demands in the classroom. Let's look at some of these demands in light of what's hardest for each of the dominant learning styles.

WHAT'S HARDEST FOR EACH LEARNING STYLE?

Auditory Learners

Difficulty 1: Not talking in class. Because of the need to verbalize their thought processes, auditory learners often don't even realize they're talking. As soon as the teacher says something that "clicks," they quickly turn to someone and talk about it. Since using other students as sounding boards is often frowned upon in traditional classrooms, the auditory learner finds comments on his/her report card such as "Needs to practice listening skills" or "Has trouble paying attention during class."

How to Help: Try talking through the issue of finding appropriate times to speak up at school. You may need to actually help your auditory children practice being quiet or verbalizing ideas to themselves before talking to someone else.

Difficulty 2: Reading silently. In order to remember what they're reading, most auditory learners prefer to read aloud. Even when they're forced to read silently, they may read more slowly simply because they're still verbalizing each and every word to themselves. Any other sounds that are made in the room while auditory students are trying to read may be even more amplified and distracting because they're already trying to listen to the sound of their own voices.

How to Help: Don't put a lot of pressure on your auditory children to read more rapidly as long as they demonstrate an adequate level of comprehension and recall. Point out how important the verbalizing is for understanding and remembering the information, realizing that sometimes this means auditory students will need to move their lips when they read.

Difficulty 3: Blurting out the answer instead of raising their hands. Since auditory learners tend to think out loud, it's difficult to stop thoughts from overflowing into speech. Often auditory students don't even realize they're talking until they're already in trouble for doing it.

How to Help: Again, helping your auditory children become aware of why this is happening and then actually practicing situations in which it can be avoided will help more than you may think.

Visual Learners

Difficulty 1: Listening to a lecture without visual aids. Despite their best efforts, most visual learners will quickly lose their concentration if they have nothing to focus on visually. At that point, just about everything becomes a distraction—posters on the wall, people walking outside in the hall, and so on. Teachers may notice these students develop a faraway look, drifting into inattention or creating a distraction among their classmates.

How to Help: Make your visual learners aware of how important it is to have something that helps them focus their imagination while listening. If the teacher does not provide what they need, help students develop coping strategies. For example, they can try drawing a picture or diagram of what the teacher is talking about, then add lines or shapes as the idea develops.

Difficulty 2: Being restricted to white paper or standard blue or black ink. Because visual people thrive on stimulating colors and textures, it's frustrating for them to confine their creativity to sterile white paper or boring colors of ink. Some teachers may become impatient with the lack of uniformity on assignment papers, thus insisting that all students be consistent.

How to Help: It often helps to let the visual child use colorful folders, envelopes, and notebooks, especially when the papers inside can't look as creative. Make a point of letting your children choose their own school materials whenever possible.

Kinesthetic Learners

Difficulty 1: Sitting still. No one fidgets and squirms better than the highly kinesthetic child! Everything from constantly changing position in the chair to actually getting up several times to walk around or go to the bathroom seems to be a normal part of a kinesthetic's day. These children can certainly drive their teachers crazy simply by maintaining an unceasing flow of energy and movement. Even when a kinesthetic child is sitting at his/her desk, some part of his/her body is usually still moving—toes tapping, head bobbing, eyes darting around the room.

How to Help: If your kinesthetic child has a teacher who is not willing to let him/her keep moving while listening or working, you'll need to teach your child coping techniques. Sometimes doodling while listening helps the child to focus. Using a highlighter to keep track of the material the teacher is talking about is also a great help. (This may mean buying a copy of the textbook for your child so he/she can write in it.) A worry stone or squishy ball will also help a child quietly squeeze out some energy without causing any trouble in class.

Difficulty 2: Doing the same thing for longer than 10 minutes at a time. Even if kinesthetic children manage to sit still and concentrate on a task, it's unrealistic to expect uninterrupted attention for more than a few minutes. The more you can keep them moving, the greater their concentration. Unfortunately, a teacher often judges how well students are listening by how quiet and still they are.

How to Help: Some teachers have agreed to let their kinesthetic pupils have more than one assigned seat. As long as they're in one seat or the other and can prove they're listening, they're not required to sit in the same place for long periods of time. If it's not possible for your child to move much at school, at least design homework and study time at home to be as flexible and movable as possible.

Difficulty 3: Looking at you when you talk to them. Robert is my highly kinesthetic son. Although he has an excellent memory and is quick to remember large chunks of data, he can't recount the Pledge of Allegiance if I make him stand still and look at me. When I let him pace, wander, and recite, he almost never makes a mistake. If I insist that he stop and focus on me, his mind quickly goes blank.

How to Help: If your kinesthetic child is getting in trouble because he/she won't look the teacher in the eye, encourage the teacher to hold the child accountable for the information, whether or not the student is standing still. If the teacher refuses to cooperate, do your best to explain to your child why it's so difficult to concentrate without moving and that it's not a reflection of intelligence.

Analytic Learners

Difficulty 1: Identifying the main idea. When they're reading or listening, analytic learners naturally pick up details. While they're busy focusing on the specifics, however, the general concept may elude them altogether. This may account for situations in which a teacher *knows* those students read the material carefully, but they just didn't *get* it.

How to Help: Because analytic learners have difficulty pulling the general from the specific, they often have trouble studying for tests. Before your child sits down to read material he/she is going to be tested on, quickly suggest two or three possibilities for the main idea. This can serve as a gentle reminder that there is an overall purpose for reading the selection.

Difficulty 2: Summarizing or paraphrasing. Since analytics are naturally prone to remember details more than trying to get a general sense of why the details are significant, asking them to put something "in a nutshell" can be extremely difficult. Questions like "What do you think this means?" can be met with perplexed stares from the analytic who is trying to figure out what in the world you're talking about.

How to Help: One of the best methods for helping analytics put a passage into their own words is to encourage them to read with a highlighter. Help them learn to highlight key words, then go back and write a summary using those words. The more they do this, the easier it will become to automatically read with the idea that summarizing will be necessary when they finish.

Difficulty 3: Answering essay questions. Many analytic students quickly and efficiently tackle the essay questions on an exam only to get the scored test back with comments like "You need to expand your ideas" or "Try giving more examples." Analytics are good at outlining and concisely stating information. However, if the teacher asking for that information happens to be more global, the answers may seem too short, the supporting statements too abbreviated.

How to Help: Encourage your analytic student to clarify what the teacher is asking for on an essay test. How many examples should be given? What kind of answer is considered too short? If the teacher will not give an answer that satisfies the analytic, try helping your child design a formula for answering every essay question. For example: (1) state your purpose; (2) give at least two reasons; and (3) write a conclusion.

Global Learners

Difficulty 1: Outlining material. Most globals struggle with the process of outlining because their minds naturally jump ahead before all the details can be covered. Since they're most concerned with getting the overall idea down, the details often show up too late, and the outline must be rewritten. Trying to write an outline of a research project or speech without knowing what the final outcome will be is almost impossible for them. Many a global has burned the midnight oil trying to write an entire paper so the preliminary outline could be handed in on time.

How to Help: One of the most effective methods for helping globals produce a formal outline is what many call "webbing" or "mapping." Start with a clean piece of paper and write the main idea in the middle. Then, in no particular order, begin to write down everything that branches out from the main idea, like limbs from the trunk of a tree. As each idea comes to mind, draw another line below the concept it should be attached to, and keep filling the page. At the end, pull out another clean sheet of paper and begin transferring the information from the web to a formal outline. You'll be amazed at how analytic the product will look!

Difficulty 2: Remembering details without knowing what to listen for in the first place. One of the scariest sentences globals can hear in school is: "Now, I'm going to read these instructions to you only once." Their minds begin to race ahead, trying to figure out what's going to happen, feeling the pressure of having to remember something really important, but not really knowing what to expect. While they're trying to figure out how to memorize what the teacher is saying, they suddenly realize the instructions have already been given and they're going to look stupid—*again*.

How to Help: Unfortunately, it may take a while before we can talk some educators into the idea that it's acceptable to repeat instructions at least one more time, especially if the listener is genuinely paying attention. Meanwhile, you can help your global learner by encouraging him/her to ask the teacher what the instructions will be *about* before they're actually given. At the very least, your global child needs to understand that missing instructions the first time does *not* indicate a lack of intelligence.

Difficulty 3: Justifying or documenting an answer. As a global learner myself, I can still remember agonizing through a math problem with no hope in sight.

Then suddenly, in a blinding flash of insight, the answer *came!* The pride and relief I felt was always short-lived, as the teacher would challenge me to show him *how* I got the answer. Since he didn't buy the blinding-flash-of-insight theory, he assumed I simply copied the answer from someone else. Because global minds operate with *chunks* of information instead of individual pieces, it's difficult for them to turn what they know into a documented, analytical format.

How to Help: It's important to reinforce the globals' sense of intuition and imagination while you're insisting they be accountable for documenting their work. Celebrate the fact that the answer came at all; then help the globals work backward to figure out what the process was.

Concrete Sequential Learners

Difficulty 1: Reading between the lines. Literature, poetry, social studies—all are among the subjects that can pose a bewildering set of questions to CS students. "Why is *The Red Badge of Courage* red?" "What does the poem *Fire and Ice* symbolize?" "Why is our flag red, white, and blue?" If the answers aren't clearly and immediately evident in the assigned material, CSs can find themselves at a standstill. My niece Kelli summed up this predicament in her typical CS manner as she pointed to the pages in her textbook: "Aunt Cindy, how can I read between the lines? There's nothing *there!*"

How to Help: If you want to help your CS learn to read beyond the written word, it will take time and patience on your part. For Kelli, her dad has probably helped her most. He'll sit down and help her define the terms of the questions, then give her some examples. He never lets her feel that her concrete mind is not intelligent enough to get it; he simply starts over as many times as he needs to until the light comes on.

Difficulty 2: Accepting interruptions or changes in routine. Sometimes something as simple as a fire drill, an assembly, or a special event can almost ruin the CS's school day. It's not that CSs don't enjoy a variety of activities; it's just that it's difficult to adjust to anything that disrupts the routine they've established. If Monday is library day and they have to skip that library time to go to the assembly, when will they go to the library? The typical random response of "Don't worry. We'll find another time to go" does nothing to reassure the CS.

How to Help: Whenever you can, try to give CSs as much advance notice as possible that their routine is going to change. One of the best ways to keep

CSs feeling secure in spite of schedule alterations is to practice some "what if" scenarios. For example: "Tom, what if you got to school tomorrow and you found out that your classroom was flooded with water?" "Susan, what if you were working in class and suddenly the fire alarm went off?" By talking through some of these situations in advance, you can prepare your CS to deal with contingencies.

Difficulty 3: Accepting exceptions to the rules. Consistency means more to CSs than the rest of us will ever realize. They have a strong internal sense of equity and fairness and will usually be the first to bring inconsistencies to your attention. Unfortunately, this often takes the form of "tattling": "Mrs. Jones! Tommy's using red ink! You said we could use only blue or black ink!" What's fair for one is fair for all, and CSs are bound to make sure that rules stay carefully enforced.

How to Help: It's especially important when dealing with CSs that you're clear about what needs to be accomplished. As long as you can demonstrate to them that the goal is being met, you'll be more successful in getting them to accept the fact that there may be many ways to get there.

Abstract Sequential Learners

Difficulty 1: Finishing assignments during class. The pressure of timed tests or short-term deadlines is probably more stressful for ASs than for any other style. ASs have a logical, systematic bent that simply can't be rushed and still be thorough enough to produce the desired outcome. Though it may seem to some of us that ASs are just dragging their feet and taking more time than necessary, it won't help to insist they hurry. We often find that ASs shut down when they feel overloaded and pressured to finish quickly.

How to Help: It may be difficult to get your AS's teacher to cooperate in giving more time to complete class assignments, but it never hurts to ask. Try to ascertain the purpose of the assignment, and propose that your AS can meet the goal even if it takes more time. If the teacher won't allow extra time, help your AS practice moving quickly through shorter assignments, giving assurance that this will not be judged as his/her best work.

Difficulty 2: Participating in cooperative learning. It's often difficult to convince ASs that working or studying together in a group would be beneficial. ASs tend to assume that the others in the group are there to act as vacuums, sucking information out of them so the rest won't have to do any work. ASs usually work most effectively when they can work independently, so they're not naturally motivated to cooperate in group efforts.

How to Help: If you can demonstrate the benefit of studying cooperatively, your AS may at least give the group process a chance. Be careful to define what the AS's role in the group will be, and emphasize that the purpose of working together is, as much as anything, to learn the *process* of teamwork.

Difficulty 3: Learning or using gimmicks, games, and so on. As a Concrete Random teacher, I found I frustrated my Abstract Sequential students when I insisted they learn the little gimmicks and memory devices instead of just presenting the information first. I was proud of myself for thinking of a great way to remember how to spell *cemetery*.

"When you were little and your mom played with your toes (this little piggy went to market, etc.)," I said, "do you remember what the last little piggy did?"

One student supplied the answer: "Cried wee, wee, wee, all the way home."

I nodded. "That's right. Well, *this* little piggy cried e, e, e, all the way through the *cemetery!*"

An AS student's hand went up, and I called on him.

"I don't understand what a pig would be *doing* in a cemetery," he protested.

I guess he missed the point!

How to Help: Encourage your AS to identify what the gimmick or neumonic device is supposed to help him/her remember. If it's not needed, don't use it.

Abstract Random Learners

Difficulty 1: Socializing too much in class. School is an intensely social experience for ARs. It's difficult to separate spending time with their friends from the learning that is supposed to happen in the classroom. The most meaningful learning that takes place for ARs is what they can share with those they care about most. Unfortunately, this "group learning" leads to comments on the report card such as "Is entirely too sociable during class" or "Needs to learn to focus on the teacher instead of his friends."

How to Help: Encourage your AR to spend time with friends outside of school, doing things that will help *inside* the classroom. For example, have a homework party—closely supervised by a parent. Instead of constantly fighting the AR's need to socialize, channel that need into productive areas that will result in better academic performance.

Difficulty 2: Following detailed instructions. One of the gifts ARs possess is intuition—a general sense of what needs to be done. It's almost contrary to that nature when the teacher insists they follow step-by-step directions to achieve a particular goal. It's particularly frustrating to ARs when the details seem so unimportant to them and yet are a priority to the teacher.

How to Help: Most ARs can succeed in fulfilling even the pickiest of details if they're properly motivated. Remembering that your AR needs to feel that he/she is doing something that will really matter, seek to find and communicate a personal sense of accomplishment. If nothing else, reinforce the fact that missing one or two details may drastically alter the overall results.

Difficulty 3: Feeling that a teacher doesn't like them. While almost all students want to feel loved and accepted by their teachers, many students can function without specifically receiving that reassurance. ARs, however, are utterly dependent on a positive relationship with their teachers in order to succeed in class. Even if social studies was Larry's favorite and best subject last year, this year it could be his worst if he believes the teacher doesn't like him.

How to Help: You may need to help ARs put things in perspective when it comes to how a particular teacher feels about them. For example, Tracy came home devastated that her name was put on the chalkboard because she was causing trouble. Tracy was sure that her teacher hated her now, and things would never be the same. Tracy's mom asked her how many names besides hers were on the board. "Well," Tracy admitted, "about 26." After Tracy and her mom discussed it, Tracy decided that it was just a bad day for her teacher, and she couldn't wait to get to school the next day and take her teacher an apology and cheer-up-I-love-you card!

Concrete Random Learners

Difficulty 1: Following someone else's rules. For most CRs, rules are really just *guidelines*. After all, rules are for people who are too stupid to do the right thing anyway! CRs often mean no disrespect; it's just that *your* rules may not seem all that necessary to *them*. Since it's common to see a list of "classroom rules" at school, it's no wonder that CRs often find themselves at odds with the teacher's system of discipline.

How to Help: Encourage your CR to discover the *reasons* for the teacher's rules. If the two of you can brainstorm together, your CR may begin to see that the rules really do make sense. Admit to the CR that certain rules may be unnecessary for some, but there is the problem of fairness and accountability. Challenge the CR to come up with some solutions that would keep everyone in class accountable within the parameters the teacher has set. (Sometimes, given the choice, the CR will simply shrug and decide it's not worth the effort to fight the rules.)

Difficulty 2: *Not being allowed to use their imagination.* The world is full of options for CRs, and limiting their choices is one sure way to quickly stir up a lot of conflict. Teachers don't always appreciate the CR's active and creative imagination when they simply want a straightforward assignment. CR responses like "This is dumb!" or "Why do we have to do this anyway?" often provoke accusations of disrespect from the teacher. It doesn't take long for the conflict to escalate to an irreconcilable power struggle.

How to Help: It's important to teach your CR the need to choose battles wisely. This may take a lot of time, patience, and trial-and-error solutions, but try to show your CR that great imagination is often wasted on petty situations.

Difficulty 3: *Investing the time and effort to master concepts and tasks.* A frequently repeated motto for CRs is "How much is really necessary?" CRs have a natural desire to conquer as much of the unknown as possible. This means they spend little or no time *mastering* concepts before moving on to new and untried territory. Of course, CRs may believe they have a grasp of a particular idea, only to find out they didn't get it right at all. Their impatience with detail and specific instructions may get them into trouble.

How to Help: It's important to get CRs committed to the outcome before you expect them to pay much attention to what it will take to get there. Remember, you can't *make* a CR want what you want, so sometimes you may just have to back off and watch the consequences unfold. For example, you may say to your CR, "Homework is half your grade in math, but you aren't doing any homework. Is a C the *best* you want to get?" If the CR says yes, you're through negotiating. You've made the outcome known, and the CR has decided it's not worth doing the homework. Now the rest is up to him/her.

MANY WAYS OF BEING INTELLIGENT

Taking hold in schools across the nation is a strong movement that uses Howard Gardner's Multiple Intelligences model.[1] As I wrote earlier, Multiple Intelligences is not a learning styles model, but it provides invaluable information on the many ways your child can be intelligent. Many fine educators have written books detailing ways to use the different intelligences for academic success in school, and there wouldn't be room in this chapter to outline all of these methods. Please refer to the annotated bibliography at the back of the book for some of my favorite resources for practical strategies using the intelligences theory.

Remember, school is often not a good measure of how intelligent or capable children are. Some of your children's traits that cause the greatest frustration to you and their teachers may end up being their best skills and abilities during the rest of their lives. I've pointed out just a few of the difficulties each of the learning styles may encounter in a typical school system. But did you notice that each of those problems is frequently caused simply by differences in learning styles? As a matter of fact, each learning style has more *assets* than drawbacks. If you help your children focus on their strengths, you'll be amazed at what they'll be able to accomplish.

Plan of Action

Using a separate sheet of paper for each of your children, write down what you see as his/her greatest success in school. Why do you think he/she is experiencing this success? Write down what you see as his/her greatest challenge in school. Why is this challenging? Talk with your child about what you wrote, emphasizing his/her strengths and how they can be used to meet challenges and overcome limitations.

Chapter Eight

Making Teachers Your Allies

By now you should be convinced that your child is a wonderfully complex and capable individual, possessing many strengths and abilities that may never be recognized or appreciated in school. Uh-oh—school. Your children must spend several years of their lives in a place that's not exactly known for being flexible and understanding when it comes to students who don't conform to the system. What can you do to make sure each of your children will be valued and nurtured? How can you effectively communicate your child's strengths to each teacher? What if your child's teacher truly doesn't care?

Many parents feel they have little control over the system that has been established to offer their children a formal education. The fact is, parents *do* have a great deal of control—but we need to use it wisely and approach our task positively.

After one of my parent seminars recently, one enthusiastic mother was eager to have me autograph a book for someone else. "I'm giving this book to my son's teacher," she explained. "I'm going to tell her she needs to *read* this!"

I winced. "Please," I said, "don't approach his teacher that way. She may *never* read the book!"

I've been a teacher in the public schools, and over the past several years, I've taught and worked with teachers and administrators in both the public and private sectors. As a result of what I've discovered in person as well as from the resources and contacts available to me, I want to assure you that most teachers care very much about their students. They are, by and large, a dedicated group of professionals who are willing to help parents in their efforts to motivate their children to succeed. But teachers have a difficult job description, complicated by the fact that most of them must deal with 20–160 students every day. Understanding learning styles does, in both the short *and* the long run, make a teacher's job easier. It *is* possible for a teacher to integrate many learning style approaches into the same classroom in practical and effective ways. Included in the bibliography at the end of this book are several resources specifically geared toward helping teachers adapt to various student learning styles.

But what happens if your child has a teacher who either doesn't know about or doesn't teach to the different learning styles? How can you tell teachers about this approach without putting them on the defensive or seeming like a know-it-all, interfering parent? I gathered dozens of trusted colleagues in the education field and posed this very question. I asked these teachers to help me give parents some tried-and-true advice for making teachers their allies instead of drawing enemy lines. I listened carefully, tabulated the written results, and the following list of suggestions represent what I believe is the best advice you'll get about communicating effectively with your child's teachers.

GENERAL CONSIDERATIONS

- Always begin by presuming the best, and treat the teacher as an expert. Assume the teacher already knows about learning styles. Take an article, book, or cassette tape and ask the teacher to read it or listen to it and give you his/her opinion.
- Know that teachers become aware of active and interested par-

ents. A teacher will usually make an extra effort to watch out for that parent's child, not because of favoritism but out of a heightened sense of awareness and personal appreciation for the child.

- Understand that with so many children in the classroom, it's difficult for the teacher to recognize and understand each child's personal learning style. Even a teacher who makes a special effort to discover and value different learning styles in the classroom fights an uphill battle with time and curriculum restraints.

- Visit the teacher under ordinary as well as extraordinary circumstances. Often the presence of a parent who comes only under negative circumstances simply puts the teacher on "red alert." Automatically, the teacher feels defensive, and the visit often starts out on a sour note.

- Don't rely solely on the information you get from your child about a particular teacher, since each person sees the world from his/her own perspective. Naturally, your loyalty rests with your child, but do your best to put the situation into perspective before talking to the teacher.

- Resolve to not be intimidated or threatened by the teacher or the school system. As a parent, your voice cannot only be heard but often carries more weight than you could imagine. This is a power you possess for good or evil—use it wisely!

- Keep in mind that a parent who takes the time to listen to both sides of an issue and investigate many alternatives can be a catalyst to constructive change. A parent who simply demands change based on a single incident or narrow view of the situation can sometimes do more harm than good.

BEFORE THE PARENT-TEACHER CONFERENCE

- Avoid phoning the teacher right after school. There are many last-minute details demanding the teacher's attention, and his/her resources may have been seriously depleted during the course of a hectic day. If possible, call in the morning before school and simply leave a message that you would like the teacher to phone you at his/her earliest convenience.

- Visualize parting from the conference with a positive feeling, even if you are seeing the teacher because of a specific problem. Don't imagine a negative ending before you talk through the issue. What's the best thing that could happen?

- Appreciate the fact that the teacher may use a completely different learning style in teaching than your child uses in learning. Be prepared to ask the teacher for suggestions for helping your child stretch his/her style to accommodate and learn from the teacher's.

- Approach the teacher with a light, easy manner; don't begin with negative comments. Be prepared to give some basic facts about your background. It may be helpful for the teacher to know what you do for a living or what educational training you may have.

- Never try to make the teacher feel inferior to you by trying to sound like you know more than he/she does. Your child deals with this teacher on a daily basis; the relationship you develop with the teacher will affect your child much more than it will affect you. Do your best to keep positive feelings between you and the teacher.

- Try to have specific concerns in mind when talking to the teacher about your child—and don't try to deal with all of them in one session. Feel free to discuss as many successes as you want, but don't try to fix all the weaknesses at the same time.

DURING THE PARENT-TEACHER CONFERENCE

- When discussing your child, include in your questions the same four words: "What can I do?" For example, "Jane's learning style is different from your teaching style. I think it's great that she's learning how to deal with many different approaches. I'm wondering, though, what I can do to help her understand the way you teach? What can I do at home that might help her succeed better in your classroom?" Let the teacher know you and your child are taking the responsibility for learning and coping with the classroom demands.

- Recognize that there are practical limitations on what the teacher can do for your child. Try to make it as easy as possible for the teacher to accommodate your child's learning style while still meeting bottom-line outcomes. For example, if you've decided that your child needs to follow a certain system for recording and keeping track of homework, make up the necessary assignment sheets so that the teacher would only need to fill in a couple blanks and sign the bottom.

- Find out what the teacher's expectations are. How does the teacher know the students are doing a good job? How is student work measured or evaluated? You may discover that a particular teacher puts more emphasis on effort than results, or that a teacher gives points for verbal participation in class discussions. Depending on your child's natural learning style strengths, these expectations may be misunderstood. Once you can define them, you can help your child understand and deal with them.

- Start and end the conference with sincere positive statements. Find the best in the situation, and build on those strengths when you find them. For example, can you tell that the teacher is genuinely concerned? Reinforce that by telling him/her how much you appreciate that concern in the first place.

AFTER THE PARENT-TEACHER CONFERENCE

- Jot a quick note of thanks to the teacher, recapping what you discussed in the way of actions you plan to take, etc. Be sure to reemphasize that you'll do your best to provide whatever support is needed.

- Discuss the conference with your child honestly and positively. Don't make it a secret, or your child may feel that you and the teacher are teaming up against him/her. Emphasize the positive aspects that both you and the teacher discussed about your child. Talk about how to use those strengths to overcome areas of possible weakness. Make sure your son or daughter wants to work on those limitations as much as you do. Unless you can agree on the goal, the methods of reaching it won't do either of you much good.

- Check back in two weeks or so, just to let the teacher know you're following up on any suggestions you have been given. Solicit any additional input or advice the teacher may have at this point.

AN IMPORTANT REMINDER

It's important to recognize, understand, and value many learning style approaches. Since your child is not just one style, a variety of teachers and teaching methods can help develop many learning style strengths. The more variety he/she experiences, the more opportunities your child will have to discover and develop natural style strengths and to use those strengths to cope with difficult academic demands. Instead of resenting a different approach, do your best to help your child understand and value a variety of methods and instruction.

Remember, every teacher is a lesson in learning for your child. By helping children discover and appreciate their teachers' unique styles, you can prepare them to face a world of differences with the confidence of knowing they can use their strengths to cope with almost anything!

IF ALL ELSE FAILS . . .

It's possible that your child's teacher simply isn't going to cooperate with you, and you'll need to take steps to switch to another teacher or even another school. This should be your last resort, but you should not hesitate to take appropriate action if it becomes necessary. The following will give you guidelines for changing your child's situation with a particular teacher or school.

- Remember, there is a chain of command. Start by talking to the teacher first about the situation and how you feel, using the advice given earlier in the chapter. Allow a reasonable time frame—usually between two to four weeks—for change to occur. Significant change is not just a day away. During this time, document your discussions and the steps you've taken with names, dates, and conversations. In both verbal and written form, make a conscious effort to control your temper and emotions. If the teacher doesn't respond in a satisfactory way, move to next level.

- Talk to a school counselor. Brief him/her on the steps you've taken and what has happened (or failed to happen). Ask for advice. If you do not receive an adequate response, move to the next level.

- Meet with the vice principal. Brief him/her on your action during the process so far and what the result has been. Be as specific as possible about your expectations and what it will take to satisfy you. Continue to document your meetings and any actions taken. If you still do not get satisfaction, move to the next level.

- Meet with the principal. Share what you've done and explain your previous meetings to prove that you've followed the chain of command. If you still aren't satisfied with the response, move to the highest level.

- Meet with the school superintendent. Be prepared to leave copies of your notes from the previous meetings, along with a written statement of your expectations. Give the superintendent at least a few days to respond to you, preferably in writing.

If all else fails, you may need to pull your child out of the school or district entirely. It is rare that you would get this far, but you need to know your options. If it's not realistic to send your child to another school and if it's impossible for you to home school, the school district needs to help you find another situation that would be appropriate for your child.

PARENTS, IT'S YOUR CONFERENCE, TOO!

Since each of us views the world from our own perspective, it's important to remember that our own learning styles will greatly influence how we respond to interactions with our children's teachers. Let's take a quick look at some suggestions for each of the Gregorc learning styles that can maximize our parent-teacher conferences.

Dominant Concrete Sequentials

- Set reasonable limits on your expectations for your child. You tend to be a perfectionist; don't let your need for detail spoil any overall success your child may be experiencing.
- Value self-worth apart from accomplishment. Don't be tempted to simply look at your child's test scores and assignments and judge success or failure without taking other elements into account.
- Be sure the teacher realizes you have feelings, too. If you let the conference focus only on the business of grades and accomplishments, you may never really convey how important your child is to you.

Dominant Abstract Sequentials

- Lighten up! If you approach the conference with an all-business attitude, the teacher may be put off from the beginning.
- Despite the fact that ASs tend to learn best by arguing, try to avoid such a tone when discussing your child with the teacher. Remember, the teacher is likely to take your criticism personally, even if you don't mean it that way.
- Try to keep your child's grades in perspective. Remember that the grade itself is usually not an accurate indication of what a student has learned. Strive to get a bigger picture from the teacher.

Dominant Abstract Randoms

- Keep the conference brief, and don't let the conversation get too personal or off track. Your naturally friendly manner will be a plus, but don't get carried away!
- Try to react less emotionally to demands made by the teacher that you believe are rigid, inflexible, or unfeeling. Point out, as logically as possible, how important it is to you that your child feels valued and loved.
- Don't expect an emotional response from every teacher. Remember, some of your child's best teachers may not express their love and appreciation the same way you do.

Dominant Concrete Randoms

- Make a concentrated effort to follow through with the good ideas you and the teacher come up with during the conference. You may have every intention of doing something at the moment, but you need to set up some means of accountability so you and your child will both stick with the decision.
- Be sure you determine how the needs of you or your child will affect others in the classroom or school. Resist the urge to insist on sweeping change; sometimes you'll need to settle for that first, small step!
- You will have more credibility with the teacher over time if you sometimes accept another's idea without always suggesting alternatives. You'll get better results if you use your need for choices and options sparingly!

Most teachers, both in public and private schools, care very much about the children they teach. Always assume the best about your children's teachers, because that means you *and* the teachers want your children to be successful. You'll quickly become allies working toward the same goals.

Plan of Action

The appendixes at the back of the book contain quick, informal profiles you can use to help describe your child to his/her teachers. There are no formal labels, but the statements and choices will provide a good starting point for discussion between you and your child, and between both of you and the teachers. Preschool and standard profiles are available. I encourage you to use these profiles as practical tools for getting a handle on each child's learning style strengths.

Chapter Nine

They Can't *All* Have ADD!

Not long ago, I attended a half-day workshop designed for parents whose children had been diagnosed with attention deficit disorder (ADD). The seminar was conducted by a reputable pediatrician who was considered an expert on ADD and related disorders, and I was curious to see what parents were being told by the medical community. About 50 parents attended, mostly as couples. I watched as they walked into the sterile conference room and sat down on cold, hard folding chairs that were placed in straight rows. Their expressions ranged from fear to frustration, and they waited nervously for the doctor to begin the instruction they so desperately hoped would give them the solution to their children's behavior problems.

As the doctor began his lecture, he immediately informed us that ADD was considered a genetic problem, and the chances were great that we as parents suffered from at least some of the same symptoms ourselves. I saw several people

105

elbowing their spouses, implying that their child must have inherited this malady from *their* side of the family. The doctor continued by stating that ADD could not be cured, and our children would struggle with this problem for the rest of their lives. I noted the despair that crossed the faces of most of the parents.

As the lecture continued, we sat stiffly in the uncomfortable chairs, watching as the doctor kept putting overhead transparencies on the screen that outlined the symptoms for those who suffered with ADD. I tried to focus on what he was saying, but I couldn't help noticing that I wasn't the only one in the room who was fighting boredom and restlessness. My biggest advantage was that I didn't have a child diagnosed with ADD. The other parents were too worried about their children to allow themselves to admit they were struggling to follow the doctor's detailed lecture.

As he displayed the list of symptoms for those suffering from ADD, I was struck by how many of them fit my learning style. In fact, my visual, kinesthetic, global, Concrete Random characteristics appeared throughout the list. Interestingly enough, the list of ADD symptoms also bore a strong resemblance to the list of qualifying traits for the *gifted* program in many school districts. I noticed many of the parents had recognized their own characteristics showing up on those lists, too, and they began to squirm uncomfortably.

As we sat for almost two hours without a break, listening to a basically monotone lecture, I couldn't help wondering why we were so surprised that children exhibit signs of boredom and attention deficit in the classroom. After all, the doctor himself had told us we were probably just as ADD as our children. Wasn't he aware of how difficult it was for *us* to sit still and listen while he lectured so relentlessly?

Throughout the four-hour presentation, I kept waiting for the moment when someone would get up and give us the *good* news. Amid all these depressing descriptions of our children's shortcomings, when would we find out what was *good* about them? I wanted to get up and tell those anxious parents about another perspective. I wanted to say, "Hey—I know your child is driving you crazy. I know the teachers are disgusted, you're frustrated, and your child is getting further and further behind in school. But the bottom line is this: *YOU'VE GOT A GREAT KID!* Every child has gifts and abilities, and we just have to help you find out how to bring out the best in each one. These children *can* succeed, even if they don't fit the traditional mold. It might be pretty inconvenient for us as parents and teachers to deal with, but there are many methods of transportation for getting our children to the same destination." But no one stood up and even *mentioned* anything positive, and at the end of the seminar I watched as the parents literally trudged out the door, despair written all over their faces.

If you're the parent of a child who has been diagnosed with attention deficit disorder, you've probably spent an incredible amount of time and effort trying to discover how you can best help that child succeed in an educational system that just doesn't fit. You've watched as this bright, capable, spirited child has struggled to concentrate and has become less and less motivated to turn in assignments or study for tests. You've dealt with the frustration of that child continually failing to follow directions and consistently showing a disregard for organization and schedules. You may have turned to both educational and medical professionals for help in identifying and prescribing a remedy so that your child can learn to cope with the discipline and structure of an inflexible and impatient world.

But how do you know which of these professionals will truly recognize the difference between your child's natural learning style strengths and an actual learning disorder? How can you be sure that your child will receive the appropriate diagnosis and treatment?

Even the most competent and understanding professional cannot provide an accurate assessment of your child until you've done your homework. It's unreasonable to expect a physician or educator to know your child better than you do. In an age when the "quick fix" has become an increasingly appealing option, you'll need to take some steps to ensure that you don't allow your child to be labeled or dismissed simply because he/she doesn't fit into the traditional educational mold.

While those in the medical and education professions are dedicated to helping your child learn to successfully cope with the world, you must be sure that the specialists you choose are also dedicated to obtaining a balanced and reasonable view of your child as an individual. How can you be certain that you're doing the best thing for your child? Start with one simple but vital step: *Know your child*.

For example, if you have a child who is a kinesthetic learner, he/she will be in constant motion. The typical kinesthetic learner needs to work in short spurts, not concentrated blocks of time. It's often easier for them to listen while they're doing something else, or to work while they're on the move. There are extremes, of course, but it's important to distinguish how much of your child's inability to concentrate has to do with a legitimate need to keep active.

A child with a more global learning style can often miss the details that a more analytic person focuses on quite naturally. While the global learner usually has a good grasp of the overall concept, it can be frustrating to try and explain analytically what he/she only knows conceptually. Again, it's important that you know how much of your child's failure to remember specific details has to do with the global or analytic bent in his/her learning style.

Please remember I am speaking as an educator and not as a member of the medical profession. For some children, medical intervention may be absolutely necessary. For others, professional counseling may be needed. For many, it will be a combination of professional help while teaching a child coping strategies to deal with tasks that are difficult.

Discipline and structure play an important part in every child's education. But I do believe it's essential that we recognize and appreciate the basic framework and design of each child's mind before we decide that there's a learning disability or attention deficit disorder. I'd like you to consider what I believe are three critical issues related to the diagnosis of and, often, medication for attention deficit disorder.

HOW DO YOU KNOW IT'S REALLY ADD?

Is there a bona fide test to determine a medical diagnosis of ADD or ADHD (attention deficit hyperactivity disorder)? I've spoken to several pediatricians and learning disability specialists. They tell me that even the leading researchers and ADD specialists can't agree on a common definition of ADD, nor can they come to a consensus on the symptoms or treatment. Thomas Armstrong, an outstanding educator and popular author, wrote in a recent article:

> I wonder whether this "disorder" really exists *in* the child at all, or whether, more properly, it exists in the relationships that are present between the child and his/her environment. Unlike other medical disorders, such as diabetes or pneumonia, this is a disorder that pops up in one setting only to disappear in another.[1]

In a related article, several educators asked an even more troubling question:

> After all, there is no definitive test for the disorder and no agreed-upon etiology. There are no blood tests to be run, no x-rays to be taken. It would seem, at least on the surface, that people generally enjoy being told by their physician that they have a clean bill of health and have nothing wrong with them; why, then, do parents wish to come away with a diagnosis of ADD for their child?[2]

Even if parents feel their child is being accurately assessed, how is the distinction made between mild, moderate, and extreme cases of ADD? How can we be sure that ADD is not being overdiagnosed or casually diagnosed if there is no conclusive medical or neurological test? The tests that determine whether or not a child has ADD must, by their very nature, be subjective. As Armstrong pointed out:

> Since these behavior rating scales depend on opinion rather than fact, there are no objective criteria through which to decide *how much* a child is demonstrating symptoms of ADD. What is the difference in terms of hard data, for example, between a child who scores a 5 on being fidgety and a child who scores a 4?
>
> Who is to decide what the final number should be based on? If a teacher places more importance on workbook learning than on hands-on activities, such as building with blocks, the rating may be biased toward academic tasks, yet such an assessment would hardly paint an accurate picture of the child's total experience in school, let alone in life.[3]

If we don't really have an accurate method of diagnosing or treating ADD, why are we often so sure it exists in so many children? What if many of the symptoms of ADD simply point out learning style differences?

WHAT'S WRONG WITH MEDICATION?

Are parents given complete information regarding possible long-term effects of taking Ritalin and similar medications? According to some of the latest statistics, "The production of Ritalin or methylphenidate hydrochloride—the most common medication used to treat ADD—has increased 450% in the past four years, according to the Drug Enforcement Agency."[4] What accounts for this alarming and sudden increase?

Ritalin is classified as a controlled substance. Are parents aware of the risks their children may be taking? The *Physician's Desk Reference* lists one of the contraindications of Ritalin as the onset of Tourette's syndrome (a disorder characterized by uncontrollable motor or verbal movements). That means that if there is any genetic predisposition toward Tourette's, the use of Ritalin could trigger this incurable disease. According to the doctors I've spoken with, there has been a general increase in the incidence of Tourette's syndrome during the past 10 years. Are parents being made aware of this?

Perhaps my greatest concern lies in the message we send to children when we are too quick or casual in prescribing medication to help them succeed. How are we teaching our children to cope with what's hard for them? Are we simply encouraging them to use mind-altering drugs as a method of dealing with difficult situations, or are we also teaching them strategies for working through their problems? Later in life, when they run into trouble again, why are we surprised that the first thing many of our children think about is turning to drugs?

HOW DO WE DEFINE "NORMAL"?

You've surely noticed by now that not everyone learns in the same way. There are so *many* ways of being smart, so *many* routes to take to reach the same destination. If you have a child who isn't experiencing success in school, don't assume it's exclusively your child's fault. After all, who decided that the only way to learn was to sit in straight rows, or listen to a teacher lecture, or concentrate quietly for long periods of time?

Let's encourage that highly active child to find ways of incorporating movement without distracting others around him/her. For example, we can teach a child to tap his/her foot without making any noise or to squeeze a rubber ball quietly while listening. Let's teach that global child some methods of turning general knowledge into specific answers on a test. Sometimes something as simple as giving several practice tests or sample questions can really help the global mind to focus on the specifics that need to be recalled on a formal exam. These coping strategies may not be the only solution for a child's learning difficulties, but they must be an integral part of any approach to improve his/her *ability* to learn.

I struggled in college to maintain a B average without having to do many boring or difficult things. When I sat in math or science classes, my mind easily strayed from the subject at hand. The homework and reading from all my college courses were overwhelming, and I often felt as if I were drowning. As I did my homework, I quickly found I was prone to distraction. At the slightest provocation, I took the opportunity to stop working and do something else. As I listened to a boring professor drone on, I usually tuned out, later finding that the information I had missed came back to haunt me at exam time. I was almost always restless, preferring to work in short spurts with frequent breaks. My level of concentration was never intense or prolonged, and I found myself regularly working on several projects at once rather than finishing one at a time. Although I could easily have been labeled as having ADHD, I didn't have it then, and I don't have it now.

You see, the interesting thing is, I found that I love to learn about everything that has to do with what interests me. I was passionately committed to becoming the best English teacher I could be, and throughout my college years and even during my graduate education, I excelled in anything that furthered my goals. I wasn't interested in expending energy to do what didn't interest or compel me. I quickly learned which hoops must be jumped through and which red tape must be cut, and I forced myself to do what was necessary to achieve my goals. I did only what was absolutely essential to get by in the subjects that had nothing to do with my life plan. My more analytic friends were horrified that I felt no remorse at getting C's or even an occasional D as long as my overall grade point average survived.

Not every child who shares my learning style will share my motivation and commitment to a goal. Even with my level of determination, I'm honestly not sure how I would have reacted if my parents and teachers had insisted I had a medical problem or learning disability. If someone had pointed out to me how unlikely a candidate I was to finish formal education and excel in my field, I'm not sure my strong-willed nature would have surrendered to their diagnosis. But what if I weren't so focused on the prize? What if I weren't really sure of what I wanted to do? Some serious self-doubt could have arisen and possibly even crippled me emotionally if I was repeatedly told I had something inherently wrong with me.

NO QUICK FIXES

There are no simple solutions when it comes to the diagnosis and treatment of learning disabilities, especially attention deficit disorder. As a parent, you should do your best to make sure your child has competent medical care and is getting an excellent education. You may have to make some difficult decisions regarding intervention and medication. You may feel defensive and frustrated when you seem to be judged by other parents who don't share your views. But remember, every child is an individual. If you've done your homework and taken the time to really know your child, you can use that knowledge to help your child become the successful learner he/she was meant to be.

When I take my children to the shoe store, the first shoes we try on may not fit. Do I change the foot or change the shoe? Of course, my children must learn to wear shoes; I can't just send them out into the world barefoot. But I must find the shoes that match the design of their feet instead of insisting that their feet conform to the design of a specific shoe. It has been my experience that when my children find shoes that fit, they wear them.

Plan of Action

If your child is struggling in school and an educator has suggested that you have your child tested for ADD, ask for a written description of the disorder and a list of the symptoms. After reading the material carefully, put a check mark by each item that you believe may be explained by your child's learning style needs. When you finish, go back and see how many items you *didn't* mark. Take your edited list to the school counselor or a trusted physician and ask what he/she thinks you're dealing with.

Chapter Ten

Celebrate Each Child!

Most police officers will tell you that movies and television shows about cops usually bear little resemblance to real life. During my six years as a police officer, however, there was one undercover investigation that played out exactly as if we were in the movies.

This assignment concerned jewel thieves and a local jeweler who was a victim in the theft of almost a million dollars' worth of uncut Australian opals. The setup was fairly simple. Our informant, a buyer, had been offered some Australian opals by a seller of questionable reputation. The informant arranged a meeting with the seller at a large hotel café. Posing as our victim's dining companions, another detective and I sat with him at a table where we could see the informant's business being conducted. Other law enforcement officers were scattered throughout the room playing various roles so our seller would believe it was simply business as usual.

115

When the seller took out his briefcase to show the opals, our victim got up and walked by that table, supposedly on his way to the rest room. We waited for a nod of his head to indicate that those were indeed his opals. When he nodded, we brought the scene to a swift and successful conclusion, arresting the perpetrator and bringing him to the police station.

As we were cataloging the evidence, I asked the sergeant if I could open the briefcase that contained the valuable jewels. *After all,* I thought, *when will I ever be able to hold a million dollars' worth of jewels in my hands again?* The jeweler watched as I eagerly opened the briefcase—only to find ordinary-looking stones.

"These are just rocks!" I exclaimed, certain we had been ripped off by someone who had substituted gravel from a driveway.

The jeweler's face registered unbelief mixed with exasperation for my inexperience. "I traveled thousands of miles to own those particular stones," he explained. "They belong to me, and I'd recognize them anywhere."

Over the next two weeks, with the help of search warrants, we found several safe-deposit boxes in which the jewel thieves had stashed hundreds of unset stones. I was amazed at the variety even within each gem family. We separated the gems by color, and when they were spread on the squad room table, free from any setting, many looked identical. Each jeweler took his/her turn sitting at the table so that individual stones could be identified and returned to their rightful owner.

I was doubtful. How could anyone search through these piles of similar stones and know for sure which ones belonged and which ones didn't? I watched as one of our local jewelers sat down and began sifting through one of the piles with a thoughtful expression on his face.

"No, this one's a stranger," he would say. Then he would pick up an identical stone and smile. "Ah, here's a friend. I remember the night I couldn't sleep because I was worried about my wife's illness. I got up at two in the morning and cut this one. See this light angle here?"

I sat in amazement as the jewelers gently and carefully reclaimed the gems that belonged to them.

As parents, we know that each of our children is a unique and precious jewel, regardless of how similar the exteriors may seem. We need to know our children as well as the jewelers knew their stones. In this book, I've offered practical ways to help you uncover your children's strengths and gifts—many you probably didn't realize were there. The next step is for us to remain focused on these strengths and gifts, because we can't build anything positive by highlighting perceived weaknesses.

Dr. Kathy Koch, in Fort Worth, Texas, has an organization called Celebrate Kids.[1] Her philosophy is that children should be celebrated for who they *are*, not just for the special days or events in their lives. It's easy to celebrate birthdays and holidays, but often we get too busy with day-to-day duties to remember to celebrate the *child*. I'd like to give you a few ideas for celebrating your children's strengths, using their natural learning styles. Practice keeping your focus on what your children do *well*, and you may be surprised at how naturally those strengths will start to overcome limitations.

WAYS TO CELEBRATE YOUR CHILD

Auditory Learners

- Help them make lists of words they like the sound of—for example, sarsaparilla, ratchet, Macadamia, Zimbabwe, and so on. Encourage them to use these words in sentences, riddles, or songs. Help them look for new words to keep adding to their lists.
- Let them surround themselves with appealing sounds (you may need to provide headsets!). Encourage them to find the music that seems to provide the best atmosphere for concentrating and working.
- Encourage them to listen to their favorite books on tape, or correlate stories with soundtracks. Point out how much sound enhances the way they remember stories.

Visual Learners

- Let them have colorful, stimulating materials and toys. Encourage them to use things that are visually appealing to help them get and stay organized in a way that makes sense and is comfortable for them.
- Challenge them to use colored pencils or ink in a way that helps what they're writing become clearer and easier to understand. Using a variety of colors can provide a welcome relief from tedious writing tasks.

- Provide as many pictures as possible for the scrapbooks that will someday chronicle their lives. Keep their childhood history books full of photographs and visual images that will capture the best parts of growing up.

Kinesthetic Learners

- Help them find as many ways as possible to keep moving in any given situation without causing disruption or misbehaving. Make it a game to come up with creative ways to use their need for movement.
- Design activities that use up as much energy as they can muster. Let them run errands, walk the dog, and deliver the paper. And don't forget to tell them how much you appreciate the steps they're saving you!
- Watch for careers that call for a lot of movement and energy. Point out the advantages of being able to stay on the move and still accomplish the task at hand.

Analytic Learners

- Ask them to help you establish short- and long-term goals for the family. Let them start the discussion with an outline of the goals they created, knowing that they'll be the starting point for a finished product used by the whole family.
- Ask for their help in figuring out what is needed to accomplish an important goal. Remember to praise their ability to sort through the details and focus on key issues and to fine-tune ideas and concepts.
- Let them help organize the family for a particular project or event. Value their ability to identify and utilize each person's skills.

Global Learners

- Let them tell you their favorite stories in their own words, feeling free to embellish by adding their own personal flair. Praise their use of imagination and creativity.
- Ask them to help you find ways to put what they're learning into action. For example, try applying a math concept to the purchase of refreshments for a slumber party.

- Help them use consensus when making a family decision. Let them know you value their ability to include all participants in the discussion.

Those High in Linguistic Intelligence

- Encourage them to use word games, including crosswords, acrostics, and so on. Let them make up their own word games, especially when creating projects around the house.
- Let them write the family's memory book, recording important observations and choosing the means of recording them (e.g., poems, videos, stories, or plays).
- Help them organize and direct a family holiday production, or let them create the message you leave on your answering machine.

Those High in Logical-Mathematical Intelligence

- Let them help you figure out the best value for products purchased, both day-to-day (such as groceries) and major purchases (such as stereos and automobiles).
- Encourage them to compute the gas mileage and the value of various transportation options on your family trip.
- Present them with challenging problems to solve that will benefit the ones they love most—for example, distributing the family chores or scheduling a particularly busy week.

Those High in Spatial Intelligence

- Encourage them to design graphs or charts to illustrate or convince the family to take action on particular projects.
- Let them play with a variety of picture games (e.g., finding the hidden object or unscrambling words).
- Encourage them to draw or doodle. Help them put their dreams on paper or paint their thoughts on canvas.

Those High in Musical Intelligence

- Challenge them to find the best background music for their various tasks (such as homework or mowing the lawn).
- Help them identify and try various musical instruments. Make

the lessons and practice fun. If they decide they don't like the instruments they've chosen, let them move on to something else.

- Let them choose at least one favorite professional musical event or concert to attend each year.

Those High in Bodily-Kinesthetic Intelligence

- Encourage "tinkering" with various projects, giving them as many hands-on experiences as possible.
- Offer gymnastics, dance, and athletic sports as early as they start showing interest.
- Praise athletic ability with or without high academic grades. Remember, their bodily-kinesthetic strengths may develop into a full-time job when they're adults!

Those High in Interpersonal Intelligence

- Give them the job of monitoring family morale and developing ideas to make everyone feel happier.
- Make them the official "encourager." Provide them with blank cards or small gifts they can choose to give to anyone who needs a lift.
- Give them lots of opportunities to entertain or work with their friends, especially when it comes to doing difficult or boring tasks.

Those High in Intrapersonal Intelligence

- Provide time and space for personal reflection and independent work.
- Encourage them to keep a journal or diary. Ensure protection from unwelcome readers.
- Give plenty of time for making decisions, especially when they involve a change of routines or comfortable methods.

Dominant Concrete Sequential Learners

- Let them help you design and implement a general family schedule or routine. Challenge them to design a format that allows for interruptions or last-minute changes without too much stress.

- Encourage them to keep track of what needs to be done during the coming weeks or months. Challenge them to remind family members of their duties in the most positive and motivating ways.
- Offer rewards for completed checklists and chores. Be specific with your praise and consistent with the consequences.

Dominant Abstract Sequential Learners

- Challenge them to find ways to constructively analyze and improve household systems or chores. Praise them for their insight and thoughtful analyses.
- Encourage them to plan ahead to allow as much time as possible to complete projects and assignments. Give them extra time to deliberate, and don't rush them unless it's absolutely necessary.
- Reward them for their efforts to meet others' expectations by letting them set and meet their own as much as possible. Since they thrive on independence, find as many ways of letting them be on their own as you can.

Dominant Abstract Random Learners

- Give them a weekly or monthly budget of time and/or money to be spent finding ways to encourage others. Value their ability to discover what people need, and help them find even little ways to meet those needs.
- Every day, find a reason to compliment them or praise them— but make your observations genuine and sincere. Remember, "No news is good news" is definitely not an AR motto!
- At the end of the day, debrief your ARs in an informal and loving way, such as over a cup of hot chocolate or a glass of milk. Ask them how they feel about their day and what you can do to help them feel better.

Dominant Concrete Random Learners

- Help them find ways to keep their day moving and full of variety. For example, whenever possible, encourage them to schedule some of their most interesting activities during the times of day that are usually the most boring.

- Challenge them to design new methods for achieving old goals, such as doing chores, taking tests, or listening quietly. As long as they demonstrate bottom-line accountability, praise them for their ingenuity!
- Ask them for their input into as many family decisions as possible, respecting their ideas—and politely declining the ones you can't live with. Let them know they're a vital part of the family and you value their participation.

YOU'VE GOT A GREAT KID!

Have you ever stopped to consider that the very traits and characteristics that annoy you most about your children may actually be the ones that may make them most successful later? If you'll start taking time to celebrate the differences between you and your children, you'll discover that your whole perspective on life may improve more than you ever thought possible!

Our children represent what we hope is our most valuable contribution to the future. What are we contributing to *them?* As you invest your love, time, and energy, consider how much that investment will grow when you nurture each child according to the way he/she is naturally bent to learn. What better retirement plan could we hope for than to see our children mature, take their places in the world, and fulfill their unique potential.

Plan of Action

Using a separate sheet of paper for each child, make a list of at least two ways you can celebrate his/her learning style strengths before the week is over.

Epilogue

Now What?

You've got style! I've got style! All God's children have got style! And you can't wait to share this with your family, friends, and colleagues. Great! Keep that enthusiasm! But before you get *too* carried away, consider the following comments and suggestions.

1. Resist the temptation to "test" everyone and categorize them according to a particular learning style label. Remember, there are *many* pieces to the puzzle. The greatest value of learning styles lies in their diversity. Don't make them seem like a prepackaged deal.

2. Identify and reinforce the *positive* aspects of a person's learning style before you try to change behaviors or perspectives. Avoid such negative references as "Well, what do you expect from a *sequential!*" Instead, make a concentrated effort to focus on the positive: "I can certainly see why your global, big-picture strengths are a real asset here!"

3. Although the learning styles theory is sound and the strategies in this book are practical, you can't always expect instant change as you implement these good ideas. Give yourself some time to observe and practice, and you'll be amazed at the difference it will make!

4. Keeping in mind that everyone will view this "learning styles thing" through their own style "screen," be sure you're practicing what you preach as you work to convince others of the importance of this approach. For example, when you're talking with:

Analytics and/or Sequentials

- Establish the credibility of learning styles research and have a list of resources and a bibliography available.
- Be as logical as possible when explaining what learning styles are and why an understanding of them can be so effective.
- Be prepared to share specific examples that demonstrate how understanding and using learning styles has made a difference in your life.
- Value each individual's learning style; do not press to "convert."
- Emphasize that *outcomes* will not be sacrificed by varying methods—bottom-line accountability always stays intact.
- Reinforce that everyone can become responsible for his/her own learning by discovering and utilizing learning style strengths.

Globals and/or Randoms

- Point out how learning styles can boost self-esteem and confidence in one's ability to succeed.
- Validate the strengths of each person's dominant learning style; don't press them to "convert" to a more traditional or analytic approach.
- Value flexibility; emphasize the importance of using many different routes to get to the same destination.
- Remind them how many ways there are of being intelligent. Even those who don't succeed in traditional classrooms can

achieve incredible success later if they understand what they do well naturally.

As you contemplate the often-daunting task of altering attitudes and transforming systems of education and learning, don't give up! Change may come slowly, but it will be parents and educators like you who will make more of a difference for your children than you could ever imagine. Each child is a complex and wonderful individual. As we're entrusted with their care, let us constantly strive to find ways to help them discover and use their natural learning style strengths to find success and make their unique contributions to the world. As parents, we have no more important task than loving our children. Let us invest our time and effort in developing those strategies that will truly bring out the best in each child.

The appendixes that follow this chapter contain valuable information and resources as you continue your journey of knowledge and application of learning styles. Appendix A has a *Plan of Action* form. Ideally, you should fill this out as soon as you finish reading this book. It will help you summarize and crystallize what you've learned. Appendixes B.1, B.2, and B.3 contain examples of informal *Learning Styles Profiles*—specifically, the standard school profile, a preschool version, and an individual profile.

Appendix A

Plan of Action

Date_____

1. As a result of reading this book, list three insights you have had about your own learning style.

2. List three things you have discovered about the learning styles of your spouse and/or children.

3. What are two goals you have for immediate change?

4. What are two long-term goals you would like to achieve either as an individual or as a family?

5. How will you know that understanding learning styles has made a difference in your family?

Appendix B.1

Communicating with Your Child's Teacher: A Student Profile (Preschool Version)

The following is based on the information in the book *The Way They Learn* by Cynthia Ulrich Tobias, published by Focus on the Family. It is designed to be a guide for parents in describing each child's strengths and preferences to a teacher. If you send a SASE to Learning Styles Unlimited, Inc., 1911 S.W. Campus Drive, Suite 370, Federal Way, WA 98023, we'll send you a reproducible copy of the following profile. *It is copyright-free in order to allow you to distribute it for personal and small-group or classroom use. It may not be sold or used commercially.*

Remember, you are *not* necessarily asking for special treatment for your child, and you are certainly not suggesting that the teacher or caregiver compromise standards or excuse your child from meeting fundamental academic outcomes. You are sharing what you know about your child and asking the teacher for insights that may aid you in helping your child understand, appreciate, and cope with demands that may or may not match his/her natural learning style.

The following should be filled out by you as you carefully observe and talk to your child.

Child's Name_____
        Date_____

I. Environmental Preferences (How Does He/She Concentrate?)

Seems most alert during which time(s) of day?

_____

When concentrating, even at play, _____(needs, doesn't
need) some sort of intake (food or drink)

Seems to be able to concentrate and play best in
_____ (bright, moderate, dim) light

II. Modalities (How Does He/She Remember?)

Is successful most often when he/she can:

_____ repeat words aloud, or turn information into a song or rhyme

_____ see a picture of what is meant, draw or cut out pictures, or use
colorful folders, stickers, etc., to organize toys or materials

_____ keep on the move, take frequent breaks, work in spurts of
great energy, shift position often

III. Cognitive Style (How Does He/She Interact with Information?)

When listening to information or directions, usually seems to
    (choose one)

_____ get the gist of things, understand the main idea

_____ remember specific details, can repeat things word for word

When being read to, often
    (choose one)

_____ doesn't mind if the story is abbreviated or paraphrased; tends
to prefer stories that hold a great deal of personal interest

_____ wants to hear every word, no variation from the original story, tends to prefer subjects that can increase knowledge

When playing or creating, usually
(choose one)

_____ prefers a variety of projects in process simultaneously; may spread materials out over several different work areas

_____ prefers to complete one project at a time; works best with a structured schedule; needs a clear and efficient work space; needs to break larger projects into manageable parts

IV. Mind Styles™ (How Does He/She Communicate What He/She Knows?)

On a day-to-day basis, prefers
(choose one)

_____ having a parent or teacher provide predictable plans and routines

_____ understanding the purpose for and having time to complete the schedule and routines

_____ knowing and doing what will make everyone else happy

_____ doing what the inspiration of the moment dictates

When it comes to responding to authority figures, seems to especially need
(choose one)

_____ clear and specific rules and expectations

_____ confidence in the ability and position of the authority figure

_____ reassurance of love and personal worth despite making a mistake

_____ to feel that the person in authority respects and seeks input on the issues

Strengths and Preferences

Which of the following are your child's favorite types of free time activities?

(check all that apply)

_____ Blocks

_____ Legos/other construction materials

_____ Puzzles

_____ Computer

_____ Books

_____ Alphabet blocks/manipulative letters

_____ Sandbox

_____ Nature/science activities

_____ Drawing, coloring, creating with art materials

_____ Outdoor play

_____ Sports

_____ Lacing/sewing cards, stringing beads, pegboards

_____ Role-playing or play-acting

_____ Playing with dolls

_____ Other _____

_____

_____

My child's favorite toys _____

_____

_____

Most often, my child prefers to play

(choose one)

_____ alone

_____ with other children

_____ with adults

Summary

Child's Name_____
          Date_____

I would consider the following to be among my child's greatest strengths:

_____
_____
_____
_____
_____
_____
_____
_____
_____

I feel my child needs encouragement in the following areas:

_____
_____
_____
_____
_____
_____

My goals for my child's school year include:

_____
_____
_____
_____
_____

Here is what I feel is most important for you as a teacher to know about my child:

_____
_____
_____
_____

_____

_____

_____

_____

_____

_____

_____

_____

_____

_____

_____

_____

_____

Appendix B.2

**Communicating with Your Child's Teacher:
A Student Profile**

The following is based on the information in the book *The Way They Learn* by Cynthia Ulrich Tobias, published by Focus on the Family. It is designed to be a guide for parents in describing each child's strengths and preferences to a teacher. If you send a SASE to Learning Styles Unlimited, Inc., 1911 S.W. Campus Drive, Suite 370, Federal Way, WA 98023, we'll send you a reproducible copy of the following profile. *It is copyright-free in order to allow you to distribute it for personal and small-group or classroom use. It may not be sold or used commercially.*

Remember, you are *not* necessarily asking for special treatment for your child, and you are certainly not suggesting that the teacher compromise standards or excuse your child from meeting fundamental academic outcomes. You are sharing what you know about your child and asking the teacher for insights that may aid you in helping your child understand, appreciate, and cope with demands in the classroom that may or may not match his/her natural learning style.

The following should, whenever possible, be filled out by you and your child *together!*

Child's Name_____

      Date_____

I. Environmental Preferences (How Does He/She Concentrate?)

Seems most alert during which time(s) of day?

_____

When doing his/her best work, _____(needs, doesn't
need) some sort of intake (food or drink)

Seems to be able to concentrate and play best in
_____ (bright, moderate, dim) light

Is almost always most comfortable doing homework

_____

(at a desk, on the floor, on the bed, or other)

II. Modalities (How Does He/She Remember?)

Is successful most often when he/she can:

_____   repeat the words aloud, drill verbally, or turn the information
into a song or rhyme

_____   see a picture of what is meant, sketch out an idea, or use colorful folders to organize materials

_____   keep on the move, take frequent breaks, work in spurts of
great energy, shift position often

III. Cognitive Style (How Does He/She Interact with Information?)

When listening to information or directions, usually seems to
(choose one)

_____   get the gist of things, understand the main idea

_____   remember specific details, can repeat things word for word

When reading, often
(choose one)

_____ reads quickly, skipping unfamiliar words or substituting words; tends to choose subjects of personal interest and fiction

_____ reads slowly and deliberately, reads every word, stopping when there is an unfamiliar word; tends to choose subjects that can further knowledge, not much light reading

When organizing, usually
(choose one)

_____ works with piles instead of files; may spread materials out over several work areas; tends to procrastinate

_____ works best with a structured schedule; needs a clear and efficient work space; needs to break larger projects into manageable parts

IV. Mind Styles™ (How Does He/She Communicate What He/She Knows?)

When learning, is
(choose one)

_____ more interested in obvious facts than in hidden meanings

_____ often interested in where a person *got* the facts

_____ most interested in the background of the person *giving* the facts

_____ mostly just interested in how much of the facts are really necessary

On a day-to-day basis, prefers
(choose one)

_____ having a parent or teacher provide predictable plans and routines

_____ designing his/her *own* schedules or routines

_____ knowing what will make everyone else happy

_____ doing whatever the inspiration of the moment dictates

When it comes to responding to authority figures, seems to especially need (choose one)

_____ clear and specific rules and expectations

_____ logical reasons for procedures and guidelines

_____ reassurance of personal worth despite making a mistake

_____ to feel the mutual respect of the person in authority and input on the issues

Summary

Child's Name_____

Date_____

Here is what I feel is most important for you as a teacher to know about my child:

_____

_____

_____

_____

_____

_____

_____

_____

_____

_____

_____

_____

_____

_____

_____

_____

_____

_____

_____

_____

_____

_____

_____

_____

_____

_____

_____

_____

Appendix B.3

An Individual Profile

The following is based on the information in the book *The Way We Work* by Cynthia Ulrich Tobias, published by Focus on the Family. It is designed to be a guide for describing your individual strengths and preferences to those with whom you live and work. If you send a SASE to Learning Styles Unlimited, Inc., 1911 S.W. Campus Drive, Suite 370, Federal Way, WA 98023, we'll send you a reproducible copy of the following profile. *It is copyright-free in order to allow you to distribute it for personal and small-group or classroom use. It may not be sold or used commercially.*

Remember, you are *not* using this to provide an excuse for not doing what is difficult or unpleasant. You are simply sharing what you know about your own style and providing insights that can help your family and colleagues understand and communicate with you more effectively.

After you have filled out one of these profiles for yourself, try asking another person who knows you well to fill one out on your behalf. It will be interesting to see if the two match!

Name_____

Date_____

I. Environmental Preferences (How Do I Concentrate?)

I am usually most alert during which time(s) of day?

_____

When doing my best work, I _____(need, don't need) some sort of intake (food or drink).

I normally concentrate best in _____(bright, moderate, dim) light.

I'm almost always most comfortable doing work

_____.

(at a desk, on the floor, on the couch, or other)

II. Modalities (How Do I Remember?)

I'm successful most often when I can:

_____ use others as a sounding board to talk through issues or plans.

_____ see a picture of what is meant, sketch out an idea, or use colorful folders to organize materials.

_____ keep on the move, take frequent breaks, work in spurts of great energy, shift position often.

III. Cognitive Style (How Do I Interact with Information?)

When listening to information or directions, I usually seem to
(choose one)

_____ get the gist of things, understand the main idea.

_____ remember specific details, repeat things word for word.

When reading, I often
(choose one)

_____ read quickly, skipping unfamiliar words or substituting words; tend to choose subjects of personal interest and fiction.

_____ read slowly and deliberately, read every word, stopping when there is an unfamiliar word; tend to choose subjects that can further knowledge, not much light reading.

When organizing, I usually
(choose one)

_____ work with piles instead of files; may spread materials over several work areas; tend to procrastinate until the last minute.

_____ work best with a structured schedule; need a clear and efficient work space; need to break larger projects into manageable parts.

IV. Mind Styles™ (How Do I Communicate What I Know?)

When taking in new information, I am
(choose one)

_____ more interested in obvious facts than in hidden meanings.

_____ often more interested in where a person *got* the facts.

_____ most interested in the background of the person *giving* the facts.

_____ mostly interested in how much of the facts are really necessary.

On a day-to-day basis, I prefer
(choose one)

_____ being provided with predictable plans and routines, specific expectations.

_____ designing my *own* schedules or routines, grasping an overall design or structure.

_____ knowing what will keep everyone happy, what will bring harmony and understanding.

_____ doing whatever the inspiration of the moment dictates, keeping lots of action in my day.

When it comes to responding to authority figures, I especially need
(choose one)

_____ clear and specific rules and expectations.

_____ logical reasons for procedures and guidelines.

_____ reassurance of personal worth despite making a mistake.

_____ to feel the mutual respect of the person in authority and input on the issues.

Summary

Name_____

Date_____

Here is what I believe is most important for you to know about me in order to understand and work with me:

_____
_____
_____
_____
_____
_____
_____
_____
_____
_____
_____
_____
_____
_____
_____
_____
_____
_____
_____

Notes

Chapter 1

1. Cynthia Ulrich Tobias, *The Way They Learn: How to Discover and Teach to Your Child's Strengths* (Colorado Springs, Colo.: Focus on the Family Publishing, 1994).

Chapter 2

1. Max Lucado, *In the Eye of the Storm* (Dallas: Word, 1991).
2. Cynthia Ulrich Tobias, *The Way They Learn: How to Discover and Teach to Your Child's Strengths* (Colorado Springs, Colo.: Focus on the Family Publishing, 1994).
3. Rita Dunn and Kenneth Dunn, *Teaching Secondary Students Through Their Individual Learning Styles: Practical Approaches for Grades 7–12* (Boston: Allyn and Bacon, 1993); and Dunn, Dunn, and Janet Perrin, *Teaching Young Children Through Their Individual Learning Styles: Practical Approaches for Grades K–12* (New York: St. John's University, 1993).
4. Walter B. Barbe, *Growing Up Learning* (Washington, D.C.: Acropolis Books, 1985).
5. Herman Witkin and Donald R. Goodenough, *Cognitive Styles: Essence and Origins* (New York: International Universities Press, 1981); Witkin, C. A. Moore, Donald R. Goodenough, and P. W. Cox, "Field-Dependent and Field-Independent Cognitive Styles and Their Educational Implications," *Review of Educational Research* 47 (Winter 1977): 1–64.

6. Howard Gardner, *Frames of Mind: The Theory of Multiple Intelligences* (New York: Basic Books, 1983).

7. Anthony F. Gregorc, *An Adult's Guide to Style* (Columbia, Conn.: Gregorc Associates, 1982).

Chapter 3

1. Cynthia Ulrich Tobias, *The Way They Learn: How to Discover and Teach to Your Child's Strengths* (Colorado Springs, Colo.: Focus on the Family Publishing, 1994).

Chapter 4

1. Anthony F. Gregorc, *An Adult's Guide to Style* (Columbia, Conn.: Gregorc Associates 1982).

Chapter 7

1. Howard Gardner, *Frames of Mind: The Theory of Multiple Intelligences* (New York: Basic Books, 1983).

Chapter 9

1. Thomas Armstrong, "ADD: Does It Really Exist?" *Phi Delta Kappan* (Feb. 1996).

2. Richard W. Smelter, Bradley W. Rasch, Jan Fleming, Pat Nazos, and Sharon Barnowski, "Is Attention Deficit Disorder Becoming a Desired Diagnosis?" *Phi Delta Kappan* (Feb. 1996).

3. Armstrong, "ADD: Does It Really Exist?"

4. Ibid.

Chapter 10

1. Kathy Koch and Celebrate Kids, Inc., P.O. Box 136234, Fort Worth, TX 76136; (817) 238-2020.

Annotated Bibliography

Here are some of my favorite and most trusted resources for learning more about learning styles.

Armstrong, Thomas. *The Myth of the A.D.D. Child: 50 Ways to Improve Your Child's Behavior and Attention Span Without Drugs, Labels, or Coercion.* New York: Dutton Books, 1995.

A former special education teacher, Dr. Armstrong provides 50 practical, positive ways to help the ADD child. His heartfelt and well-researched position is that ADD doesn't exist and that the children who experience behavior and attention problems are healthy human beings with a different style of thinking and learning.

_____. *7 Kinds of Smart.* New York: Penguin Books, 1993.

Using Howard Gardner's model of Multiple Intelligences, Armstrong provides easily understood descriptions of the seven intelligences, as well as a list of 25 ways to help your child develop each one.

Barbe, Walter B. *Growing Up Learning.* Washington, D.C.: Acropolis Books, 1985.

Although this book is currently out of print, you'll find your trip to the library to read it well worthwhile. The former editor of *Highlights Magazine* shares a wealth of information about auditory, visual, and kinesthetic modalities. You'll find age-appropriate checklists and dozens of suggestions for helping your child learn in many different ways.

Breggin, Peter R., and Ginger Ross Breggin. *The War Against Children: How the Drugs, Programs, and Theories of the Psychiatric Establishment Are Threatening America's Children with a Medical "Cure" for Violence*. New York: St. Martin's Press, 1994.

Dr. Breggin is a psychiatrist who has taken a stand against the use of medication for social control of children and their behaviors. He and his wife have written this compelling book, providing a host of alternative measures for fulfilling the genuine and often inconvenient needs of children.

Butler, Kathleen. *It's All in Your Mind: A Student's Guide to Learning Styles*. Columbia, Conn.: The Learner's Dimension, 1988.

Using Anthony Gregorc's model of learning styles, Dr. Butler has written a workbook designed to be used with teenagers who want to identify and learn to use their learning styles to be better students.

Chess, Stella, and Alexander Thomas. *Know Your Child*. New York: Basic Books, 1987.

This volume is packed with evidence (including longitudinal research studies) to prove that children have their own, unique temperaments from the beginning to the end of life. The authors' "goodness of fit" theory has some practical applications to successful parenting.

Gregorc, Anthony F. *An Adult's Guide to Style*. Columbia, Conn.: Gregorc Associates, 1982.

This is the definitive volume for identifying and understanding Gregorc's model of learning styles. Packed with definitions and examples, this book is an invaluable reference for serious study.

Keirsey, David, and Marilyn Bates. *Please Understand Me: Character and Temperament Types*. Del Mar, Calif.: Prometheus, Nemesis, 1978.

This book provides a fascinating look at personality types and temperaments. You'll discover how your temperament affects your success in relationships, careers, and life in general.

Kroeger, Otto, and Janet M. Thuesen. *Type Talk*. New York: Delacorte Press, 1988.

This is a fun, easy-to-read guide to the Myers-Briggs version of Carl Jung's personality types. Loaded with anecdotes, this book is one you'll find yourself loaning to your friends.

Rusch, Shari Lyn. *Stumbling Blocks to Stepping Stones*. Seattle: Arc Press, 1991.

This book relates the touching, true story of a little girl growing up with multiple "learning disabilities" who struggled to become successful in spite of a school system that gave little or no help. Full of hope as well as specific suggestions for other children who may be suffering, this book is a valuable resource for parents and teachers.

Swindoll, Charles R. *You and Your Child: A Biblical Guide for Nurturing Confident Children from Infancy to Independence*. Nashville: Thomas Nelson Publishers, 1990.

Charles Swindoll has written a compelling and eye-opening book for parents who want to instill lasting moral and spiritual values in their children. Using a scriptural perspective, Dr. Swindoll presents a powerful argument in favor of each child's individuality and value.

Tobias, Cynthia Ulrich. *The Way They Learn: How to Discover and Teach to Your Child's Strengths*. Colorado Springs, Colo.: Focus on the Family Publishing, 1994.

This entertaining and practical book should be required reading for any parent or teacher who truly wants to help their children succeed. These concepts are powerful tools for bringing out the best in a child.

——————————. *The Way We Work: A Practical Approach for Dealing with People on the Job*. Colorado Springs, Colo.: Focus on the Family Publishing, 1995.

This is an enlightening and easy-to-read resource for developing more efficient communication with coworkers. It provides a powerful plan for transforming your on-the-job relationships.

Tobias, Cynthia Ulrich, with Nick Walker. *"Who's Gonna Make Me?" Effective Strategies for Dealing with the Strong-Willed Child*. (45-minute video) Seattle: Chuck Snyder and Associates, 1992.

This video presents practical, hands-on strategies for bringing out the best in your strong-willed, Concrete Random child. This is one you'll definitely loan to your friends.

Favorite Children's Books

Brown, M.K. *Sally's Room.* New York: Scholastic, Inc., 1992.

Here is an ageless story for any parent who has fought repeated battles over a messy room.

Hazen, Barbara Shook. *Even If I Did Something Awful.* New York: Aladdin, 1992.

This is a story of unconditional love without compromising parental authority. Good for all ages!

Henkes, Kevin. *Chester's Way.* New York: Puffin Books, 1988.

This delightful story shows children how their learning style differences can help them appreciate others for their strengths.

Lester, Helen. *Tacky the Penguin.* Boston: Houghton Mifflin, 1988.

Here is a wonderful story for any child or adult who needs to be reminded that being an individual definitely has its advantages over simply running with the pack.

For more information or to obtain a speaker, please contact:

Learning Styles Unlimited, Inc.
1911 S.W. Campus Drive, Suite 370
Federal Way, WA 98023
Phone: (206) 874–9141
Fax: (206) 952–4635
email: lsu@halcyon.com

More on Learning Styles from Cynthia Ulrich Tobias!

The Way They Learn

No two kids are alike—not even identical twins. So it's really no surprise that many children struggle with rigidly structured classrooms. Unlock their potential by using each child's natural strengths and interests to enhance his or her education. By putting to work the practical approaches found in these pages, you'll eliminate much of the frustration that comes from a mismatch in learning styles (yours and theirs), and you'll stimulate their learning in ways you never imagined.

The Way We Work

Pristine offices, cluttered desktops, and everything in between . . . every employee is unique, so a one-size-fits-all approach to doing the job doesn't get the job done. Release your full potential by understanding the way *they* work. Once you identify the learning styles of the people you work with, you'll better know how to pose questions, assign tasks, and avoid buttons that shouldn't be pushed. You'll also increase efficiency, boost morale, and improve the "likeability" of some of your company's finest employees—including yourself.

Pick up either of these popular books at your favorite
Christian bookstore.